I0491024

ART BOOKS

FROM CRESCENT MOON PUBLISHING

Leonardo da Vinci
by James Pearson

Early Netherlandish Painting
by Rosalind Mutter

Piero della Francesca
by Naomi Haskell

Giovanni Bellini
by Julia Davis

Eric Gill: Nuptials of God
by Anthony Hoyland

Minimal Art and Artists In the 1960s and After
by Laura Garrard

Postwar Art
by George Knighton

Vincent van Gogh: Visionary Landscapes
by Stuart Morris

Max Beckmann
by Stuart Morris

Egon Schiele: Sex and Death in Purple Stockings
by D. Simon Eade

Mark Rothko: The Art of Transcendence
by Julia Davis

Jasper Johns
by L.M. Poole

Brice Marden
by Laura Garrard

Frank Stella: American Abstract Artist
by James Pearson

TURNER

FIVE LETTERS AND A POSTSCRIPT

TURNER

FIVE LETTERS AND A POSTSCRIPT

C. LEWIS HIND

CRESCENT MOON

First published 1907. This edition © 2020.

Set in Book Antiqua 10 on 14pt.
Designed by Radiance Graphics.

Thanks to the authors and publishers quoted.

British Library Cataloguing in Publication data

ISBN-13 9781861716101 (Pbk)

CRESCENT MOON PUBLISHING
P.O. Box 1312, Maidstone, Kent, ME14 5XU
Great Britain, www.crmoon.com

CONTENTS

NOTE ON THE TEXT

The text is from *Turner* by C. Lewis Hind, published by T.C. & E.C. Jack, London and Frederick A. Stokes, New York, 1907, as part of the Masterpieces In Colour series, edited by T. Leman Hare.

The illustrations discussed in the book are included in the illustrations section, along with many other works.

Photographs of Turner's works taken recently (by J.M. Robinson) have been included .

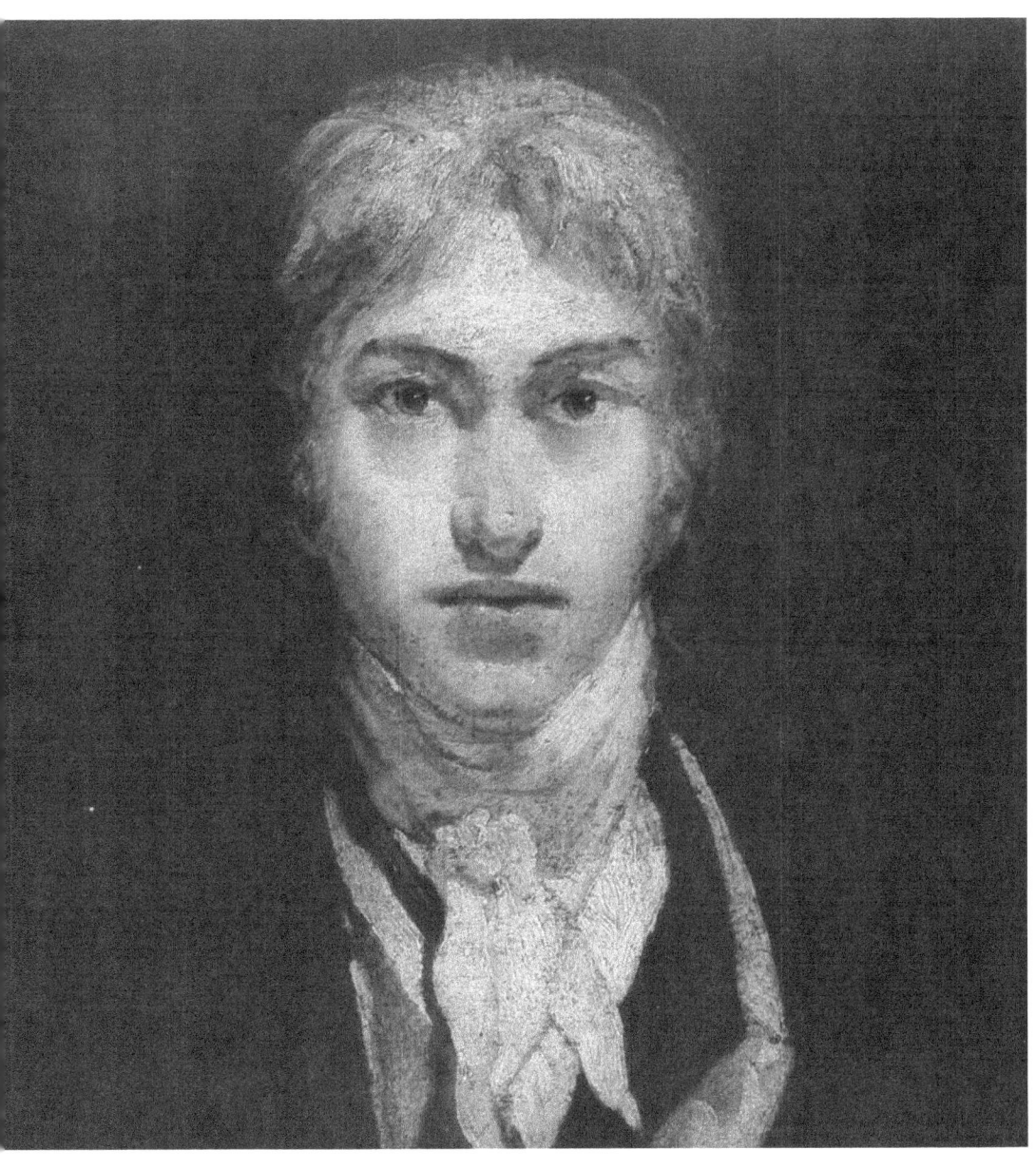

J.M.W. Turner, Self-Portrait, c. 1798, Clore Gallery

J.M.W. Turner, Norham Castle, Sunrise, 1845, Clore Gallery

LETTER I

EXPLANATORY

Yes: I remember that morning at Exeter when I surprised you making a drawing of the west porch of the cathedral. Timidly were the unrestored figures of angels, apostles, prophets, kings and warriors – very old, very battered – taking form in your sketch-book: timidly, for even then you were beginning to be troubled by the blur that rose, after an hour's work, between your eyes and the carven kings and saints.

Your sister passed into the cathedral to her devotions carrying white flowers for the altar: we stayed in the sunlight. I cannot remember how Turner became the subject of our talk; but I think it was my mention of his drawing of the west front of Salisbury Cathedral done when he was twenty-three – one of the set exhibited at the Royal Academy in 1799, which hastened his election to an Associateship of the Royal Academy. Those were the days of the tinted architectural drawings, but in that magnificent Salisbury, the details indicated, yet not insistent, the old stones yellow in the sunshine, grey-blue in the shadow, Turner was already on the track of Light, the goal of his art life. He had not yet formulated any principle, that was not Turner's way; but those small, bright eyes of his had already perceived that there is light in shade as in shine. Girtin, that marvellous boy, his friend and fellow-student, was still alive; but art was in a poor state in England, in 1799, and we can well believe that this drawing of Salisbury made Turner a marked man. I could dispense with the lamp-post boys playing with hoops, as indeed with every figure in every picture by Turner. But he needed such strong foreground notes, and he, like the older landscape painters, troubled little about figures. Claude used to say, with a laugh, that he made no charge for them. Their use was to throw back the middle distance.

Then we talked of Turner's water-colours. Had he never composed the "Liber Studiorum"; never produced gorgeous dreams of glowing colour in his oil pictures; never with veils of luminous paint flashed sunrise upon white canvases; never done a moonlight, or white sails billowing over a wet sea, he would, in his water-colours, have earned the title of father of modern landscape and of Impressionism.

You, who had seen nothing of Turner's work except the plates, good in their way, but far from being the real thing, in Mr. Stopford Brooke's edition of the "Liber Studiorum," hinted that you found the master old-fashioned. Corot, Monet, and Harpignies were your idols in landscape. That was not strange when I consider that your childhood was spent in Jersey, and your youth at Moret and in Paris, and that on your twentieth birthday, a few months ago, you were articled to an architect of Exeter, your France-loving father's native place. So the Master seemed old-fashioned, did he? And you were a little sceptical of my enthusiasm.

"Ah," I said, "if you could see a range of Turner's water-colours from the first boyish drawing of Lambeth Palace exhibited at the Royal Academy when he was fifteen, through the plodding period of his development, cumbered with ungainly figures, but set in the Turnerian air and against infinite distances, as in the winding Thames from Richmond Hill, ever moving towards the light, on to his later visions when buildings, hills, and clouds shimmer in iridescent vapour! Then the figures of men and women disappear, and after fifty years of observation of Nature those old eyes see only the chromatic glories of the reflections and refractions of imponderable sun-rays. The lovely colours linger so delicately on odds and ends of paper that it seems as if a breath must blow them away. If you could see the sapphire, opal and amethyst tenderness of his 'Study on the Rhine,' the misty hills rainbow-tinted, the sun flushing the steep castle rock and making a golden pathway over the sea, you would feel that this barber's son, morose, mean, in whose muddled brain moved until his last day magnificent ideas, has given to the world the whole history of water-colour, from the tinted drawing, to the flame of an effect seen and caught in a moment of ecstasy."

You were still sceptical! I acknowledge that there were others in Turner's day who also broke new paths – Cozens, and of course Girtin, of whom Turner is reported to have said, "Had Tom Girtin lived I should have starved." As an old man he would mumble of "Poor Tom's golden drawings." I acknowledge that since Turner's day the channel that he flooded has broadened and gushed forth into many tributaries; but he was the first, modelling himself on Claude, to start in pursuit of the sun, to break the rays, and flush the land.

I quoted a Frenchman, M. le Sizeranne: "All the torches which have shed a flood of new light upon Art – that of Delacroix in 1825, those of the Impressionists in 1870 – have in turn been lit at his flame."

I quoted Constable – generous Constable – "I believe it would be difficult to say that there is a bit of landscape now done that does not emanate from that source."

I quoted Pisarro, telling how during the war of 1870 he and Monet came to London, studied Turner at the National Gallery, and found in Turner and Constable "practical certitude in matters of technique which they had but vaguely suspected and discussed at the Café Guerbois." What would they have said had they known that Ruskin, the champion of Turner, the foe of

Impressionism, when, in 1856, he sifted the nineteen thousand Turner water-colours, drawings, studies, and the "unfinished" paintings, had condemned the sunshine and atmosphere canvases now in the Tate Gallery to half a century of obscurity, because in his opinion they were "unfinished." Turner purposely left them unfinished and elusive as sunrise itself, momentary impressions of the glory of the world. The sun is new each day, ever uncompleted: so are these records of the flame of Turner.

"They are golden visions," said Constable, speaking of the Venice pictures, "only visions, but still one would like to live and die with such pictures."

Turner, to whom the world of men and women was a place to escape from, brooded on scenes that open a pathway to tired eyes leading away somewhere west of the sun and east of the moon; he loved distances, lakes that feel their way round hills to infinity, and sunsets that are a world in themselves. Even in his dark "Calais Pier" he must open the inky clouds to a blue sky swaying above the bituminous sea. In the "unfinished" "Chichester Canal" you may sail over that happy waterway, beyond the spire, on and on whithersoever your fancy leads; in the "unfinished" "Petworth Park" you may tramp away with the hunter and the hounds past the sentinel trees to that vast sky flaming and beckoning; in the "unfinished" "Norham Castle Sunrise" the poet-artist dreamed the mystery of dawn, and as he saw the miracle unfolding, he told his dream to you and to me; he saw the blue mists parting before the sun-rays rising behind the castle; saw the opalescent sky reflected in the water; saw, perhaps, in the mind's eye, the strong red note that the picture needed, and quickly set that cow standing knee-deep in the shallows. Turner gave all of himself to the making of this lovely impression, for Norham Castle, which he drew and painted so often, was his mascot. Sketching on the Tweed with Cadell, the Edinburgh bookseller, as they passed Norham Castle, Turner suddenly swept off his hat to the ruins. "I made a drawing of Norham several years ago," he explained. "It took; and from that day to this I have had as much to do as my hands could execute."

There, I remember, I paused, noting that you were again passing your hands about your eyes. Troubled, you said that the blur had returned, and that you must work no more that day. So we walked towards the river.

On the way we saw Italian workmen in blue trousers paving a road from cauldrons of molten asphalt. We watched the little flames leaping from the bubbling mass, and I drew from the sight an image of the art life of Turner: how he stoked his furnace with Poussin, Vandevelde, and de Loutherbourg, and so brought to life his dark early works such as "The Shipwreck" and "Calais Pier"; how as he fed his fire with Claude, Crome, and Wilson the furnace glowed, and the world saw the ardour of "Ulysses Deriding Polyphemus," and the splendour of "Dido Building Carthage"; then when the flames leapt towards the sky there was pure Turner, the Turner of the "Téméraire" and the Venice dreams, a "Hastings" that has lost all earthly form; a dream boat passing between Headlands at Sunrise, and the later water-colours – the red Rigi, the blue Rigi, the blue and gold "Arth from the Lake of Zug," the moonlight Venice, and the atmospheric magic of the Lake of Uri.

When we regained the Cathedral close we met your sister returning from her devotions. She said: "What have you been discussing this summer morning?"

"I have been discoursing on The Flame of Turner," said I.

"Ah!" said she, "there's a Turner in the Museum here."

We went to the Museum and stood before "Buttermere Lake, with a part of Cromach. Water, Cumberland – a Shower." You were silent. What a catastrophe – after my dithyrambs about the flame of Turner and his slow soar to light, that I should show you, as your first Turner, that work of his early stoking period, painted at twenty-two, before he learned the method of oil painting and the ways of the sun. The lake has almost gone, the trees have blackened, only the rainbow dimly lingers. The flame of Turner? The chrysalis husk of Turner!

❖ 17

That poor "Buttermere Lake" is still the only picture by Turner that you have ever seen. And now that you are far from here, walking and digging in Sparta, and sailing in insecure little crafts to the Islands, I hold it a duty to write you in detachments this interminable letter explaining as well as I can what I mean by the Flame of Turner. Your sister will read the letters to you, ill-starred student, who, at the beginning of your art career, must not use your eyes for twelve months on penalty of blindness.

When, after the last visit to the oculist, you hurried from the lawyer's office in Lincoln's Inn Fields, where I witnessed your Will, I did not tell you that a few yards away rests a glorious. Turner, "Van Tromp's Barge entering the Texel" and sailing in golden pomp eternally through the Soane Museum. I saw it on my way to your lawyer's office. The picture is alone and I was alone with what Turner loved – a sportive sea, an arching sky, gold overhead, gold on the water, and a ship sailing home golden-hulled beneath golden sails, with flags flying at the mast, and a cunning wraith of indigo cloud sweeping down the sky to give the glamour value. You did not see the golden Van Tromp. I had not the heart to show it to you.

Now you are far from Turner. I can follow your track to Olympia, and along the path by the wood, above the excavations, to a rough sign-post, where I stood two years ago and read the words "To Arcadia!" Somewhere beyond Arcadia you are, and some day these letters will fall, one by one, into your hands.

LETTER II

HIS LIFE: AN IMPRESSION

Once in our walk from Exeter Cathedral to the river you paused and asked what kind of a man was this amalgam of poet-artist and suspicious tradesman. And I, who had been so long studying his works, and dipping into the lives of him by Thornbury, Hamerton, Cosmo Monkhouse, Sir Walter Armstrong, Mr. W. L. Wyllie, and others, tried to give an impression of the man Turner – a blur of his sayings, letters, habits, and the comments of his biographers. Some of them have bewailed that his was not a pattern life, such as would edify a Y.M.C.A. audience. Nature produces such useful lives by the hundred thousand: she makes but one Turner. The Church had blessed neither his union with Mrs. Danby, nor with Mrs. Booth, and, in his later days, he preferred rum and water with sea-faring men in Wapping or Rotherhithe to dreary dinner-parties in dreary houses in the West End of London, which does not seem to me strange. We must take him as he was and be grateful. It was Nature's whim to link this great artist-soul to the starved soul of a petty tradesman. As an artist he is with the immortals: as a man he was true son of the covetous, kindly barber of Maiden Lane, Strand, keen on halfpennies, a driver of hard bargains. The father haggled with his customers, the son with engravers and picture buyers. Secretive, suspicious, ambitious, sometimes mean, yet capable of great kindnesses and sacrifices, was this little hook-nosed man in an ill-cut brown coat, and enormous frilled shirt, with feet and hands notably small. Kind? Yes. Did he not in the Academy of 1826 cover his glowing picture of "Cologne – The Arrival of a Packet Boat – Evening" with a wash of lamp-black, because it "killed" two portraits by Sir Thomas Lawrence hanging alongside. "Poor Lawrence was so unhappy," said Turner. "The lamp-black will all wash off after the Exhibition." But Turner's moods were capricious. Like all blessed or cursed with the artistic temperament, the mood of the moment usually governed his actions. Six years after the lamp-black incident he had a grey picture hanging beside Constable's "Opening of Waterloo Bridge," and Turner (you may imagine the fury in his bright eyes) watched his brother artist heightening with vermilion and lake the decorations and flags of his City barges. Presently, when Constable had gone away, Turner put a round daub of red lead upon his grey picture, which he afterwards shaped into a buoy. Constable said when he returned, "Turner has been here and fired a gun." Turner liked a joke, and if it was sometimes at the expense of another, that was but the way of his class.

From first to last he loved but one thing with heart and soul – his art. His affection for his father, and for Mr. Fawkes of Farnley Hall, were but interludes in his passion to interpret Nature, to make her conform to his visions, and to excel his predecessors and contemporaries. Certainly, in his way, he loved his "old dad," who lived with him until his death, looking after the picture gallery of unsold works in Queen Anne Street, and helping in the preparation of. his canvases. Of his father he was wont to chuckle, "Dad taught me nothing except to save halfpence." The death of the old man was a great blow.

The love affair which Thornbury relates amounts to nothing – no human thing ever really interfered with his art. His schooling at Brentford and Margate was infinitesimal – but for a landscape and sea painter, what education could have been better than the river and the boats at Brentford and the sea and ships at Margate. He remained illiterate to the end. When he wrote a description of St. Michael's Mount for the publication called "Coast Scenery," Coombes complained that "Mr. T – – 's account is the most extraordinary composition I have ever read; in parts it is absolutely unintelligible." As Professor of Perspective at the Royal Academy he was unable to express his ideas, but, says Thornbury, "he took great pains to prepare the most learned diagrams."

Throughout his life he extended and amended that amazing poem called "Fallacies of Hope," portions of which he tagged to his pictures in the Royal Academy Catalogue. It is doggerel with occasional glints of the beauty, pomp, and wonder of the world that showered when he used his rightful methods of self-expression – eye and hand. The romance of the ancient world of myth and architecture tingled in this secretive, slovenly, Jewy man; but when he essayed to learn Greek, in the happy days at Sandycombe, the attempt had to be abandoned. The slow brain could not master the verbs.

Ambition was strong within him. No toil was too long or too severe. He travelled England and Europe, sketched everything, stored the forms of buildings and effects of light and colour; and could recall what he had garnered at an instant's notice. In painting he pitted himself against the dead, against his contemporaries, against twenty miles of country, against the very glory of the sun, wrestling with each in turn, and chuckling as they succumbed.

He saved his money and in later years hoarded his pictures. He refused to pass potential purchasers to his studio, but Gillott, the pen-maker, bearded the lion in Queen Anne Street, pushed past Mrs. Danby, joked with the old man when he growled, "Don't want to sell!" and carried off in his cab some five thousand pounds worth of pictures.

Turner re-bought his canvases when they came up for sale at

Christie's, worked without cessation, practised all manner of petty economies, and finally left his pictures to the nation and his fortune of one hundred and forty thousand pounds to found a home for "decayed male artists of English parents and of lawful issue, with an instruction for a Turner medal at the Royal Academy, and a monument to himself in St. Paul's Cathedral."

The will with its four codicils was a bewildering document. For years it was wrangled over in the courts, and in the end a compromise was effected. The fortune went to the next of kin, the pictures and drawings to the nation, and twenty thousand pounds to the Royal Academy. Ruskin summed up the compromise thus: "The nation buried, with threefold honour, Turner's body in St. Paul's, his pictures at Charing Cross, and his purposes in Chancery."

If Turner, as he eyes the landscape of the Elysian Fields, retains aught of earth-life frailty, he must look angrily down upon the Turner. section of the National Gallery, upon the rooms beneath, reached by a winding staircase, where some of his water-colours are crowded, upon the sunlight canvases at the Tate Gallery; and at certain provincial exhibitions whither some of his works have overflowed from the National Gallery. For he stated explicitly in his will that the pictures should be kept together in a room or rooms to be added to the National Gallery, to be called Turner's Gallery, and to be built within ten years of his demise.

I still hope that the Turner Gallery may be built. Perhaps the hope will become a reality. What a sight Turner's pictures chronologically arranged would be, from the dim experimental pieces and the "Moonlight: A Study at Millbank," to those four works, splendid failures, now at the Tate Gallery, that he painted the year before he died, when the mind of the old man, having flamed from the embers to express the opalescent loveliness of Venice, the grey tumult of the sea in the Whaling series, the glory of the sun flashed in stains of luminous colour upon white canvases, harked back, in the shadow of death, to the old legends he had always loved, and painted them as of yore, but now blurred and tumbling, mighty ruins rising from blue lakes by great rivers and arching pines, with an impossible Æneas relating his story to an unrealised Dido, or being admonished by a Noah's-Ark Mercury. The imagination remains gorgeous if chaotic; at seventy-five he still reaches towards the unattainable, still seeks in visions a way of escape from the materialism and stupidity of the world.

What a triumph to see the range of oil pictures with the water-colours stepping daintily through the stages of his development to those latter dreams of the Rhine and Swiss lakes, fairy scenes that live, as by a miracle, on pieces of mere paper; also the proofs of the "Liber," with Mr. Frank Short's interpretations of the drawings that were never engraved, bringing the number up to a round hundred; also the tall books, one cold, beautiful steel engraving on a page, such as "Château Gaillard" in the volume called "Turner's Annual Tour, 1834," a view which charms the eyes dulled by grey London and makes the feet impatient to be off to Richard Coeur-de-Lion's castle on the bend of the Seine. The portraits, sketches and caricatures, too, of Turner of Maiden Lane, Hand's Court, Hammersmith, Twickenham, Queen Anne and Harley Streets, Chelsea, and of all the world – they should hang near his life-work.

You will see him, when the good time of the Turner Gallery comes, as a pretty youth, painted by himself, no doubt a flattering likeness, which hangs in the National Gallery. It is a bust portrait, full-face, with large estimating eyes, somewhat amazed, a heavy nose, and a dropping under-lip. An attractive boy; but you must remember that Turner the idealist painted it, and that he had worked for a time in the studio of Sir Joshua Reynolds.

Nearer to the Turner that one visualises is the sturdy middle-aged man seated under a tree, cross-legged, pencil in hand, in the painting by Charles Turner. The brickdust face is clean-shaven, the nose unmistakably Semitic; the hair is long, and the whiskers straggle to the collar. A drawing rests upon his knee; he looks forth with an eye like a sword, considering how he shall change the landscape. The sketch by Maclise is a delight. Turner sits on a stool up in the clouds, painting; the tail of his coat flaps over towards the earth, his boot is crooked into the support of the easel, and beneath him rises the sun with the word "Turner" blazoned amid the rays. But the best of the series, because it has that touch of caricature which often approaches nearer to life than a reasoned drawing, is the portrait by William Parrott made on Varnishing Day at the Royal Academy in 1846, when he was seventy-one. Turner is painting furiously upon his picture. The frame stands on the floor. The top is but an inch shorter than the battered beaver hat crushed over upon his big head. His Mrs. Gamp umbrella leans against a chair. His fellow-Academicians stare at his picture and at his colour-box, puzzled. "How does he do it?" they whisper.

In those days the members of the Academy were allowed four varnishing days. In his latter years Turner would send his pictures merely laid in with white and grey and complete them on the varnishing days. There was brown sherry at luncheon, and Wilkie Collins describes the old man as "sitting on the top of a flight of steps, or a box, like a shabby Bacchus nodding at his picture." But he could paint a "Rain, Steam, and Speed" and "The Sun of Venice going to Sea" in spite of the brown sherry, and his lonely bachelor life.

But brown sherry or no brown sherry, to his dying day he never lost interest in the love of his life, light. At seventy years of age, when he is described as stooping, looking down and muttering to himself, he would pump Brewster as to all he knew on the subject of light. Those were the days of the infancy of photography, and Mr. Mayall, who was experimenting with daguerreotypes, tells how the old man, whose eyes were then weak and bloodshot, would sit in his studio day after day asking questions. He pretended that he was a Master in Chancery.

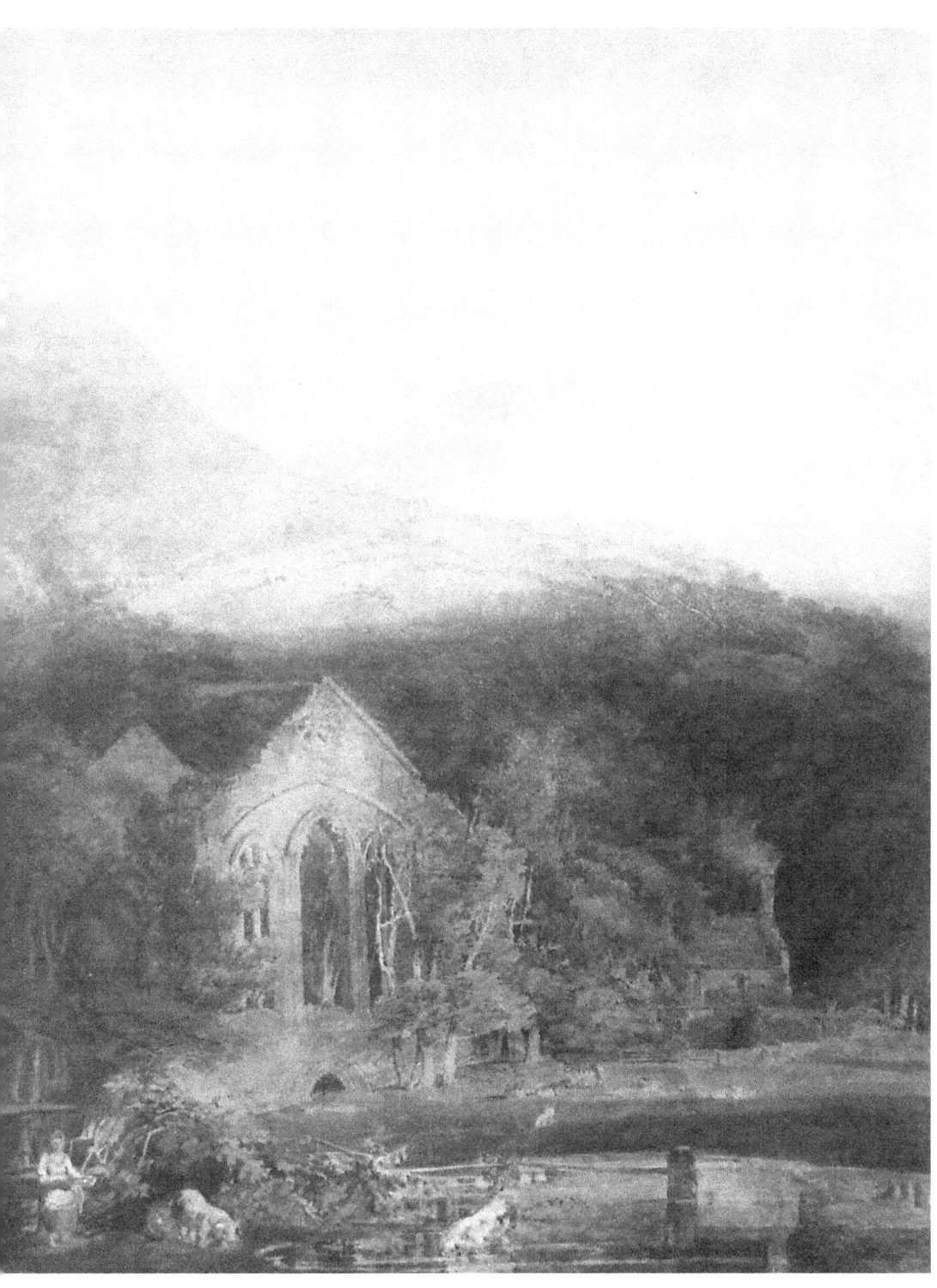

J.M.W. Turner, Dinas Bran, 1795, Clore Gallery

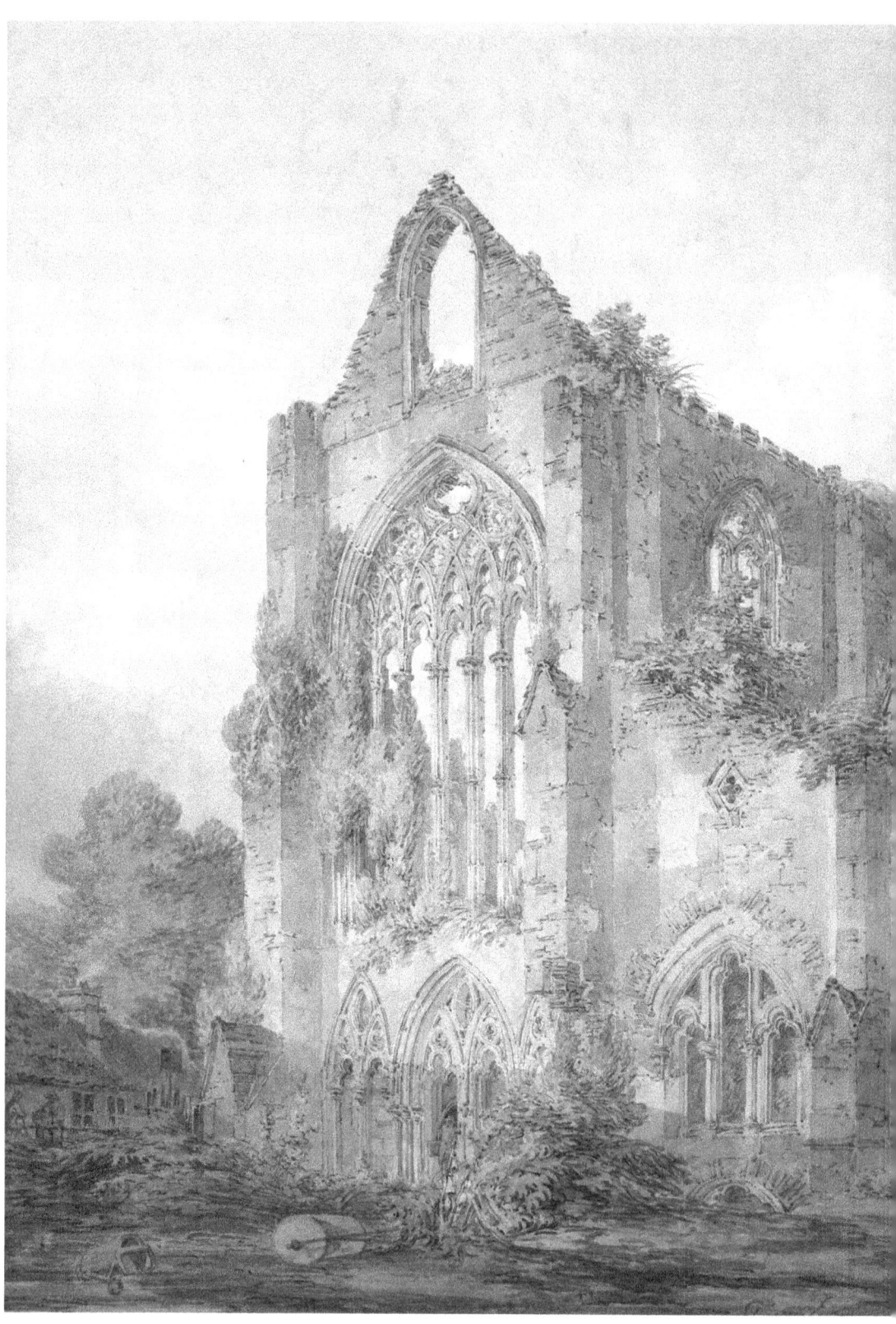

J.M.W. Turner, Tintern Abbey, British Museum

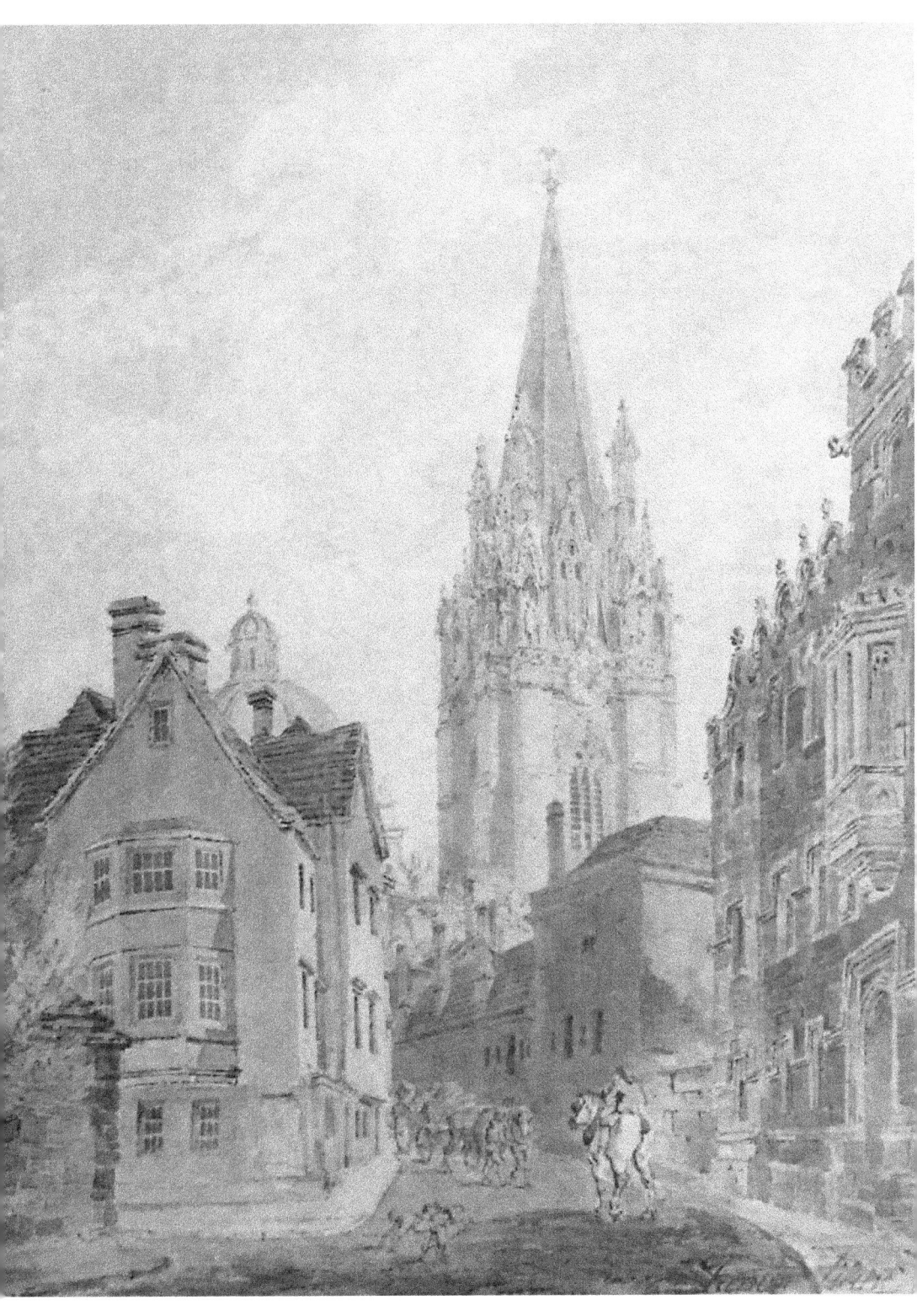

Jude Fawley's beloved Oxford:
J.M.W. Turner, Oxford: St Mary's From Oriel Lane, 1793,
Clore Gallery, London

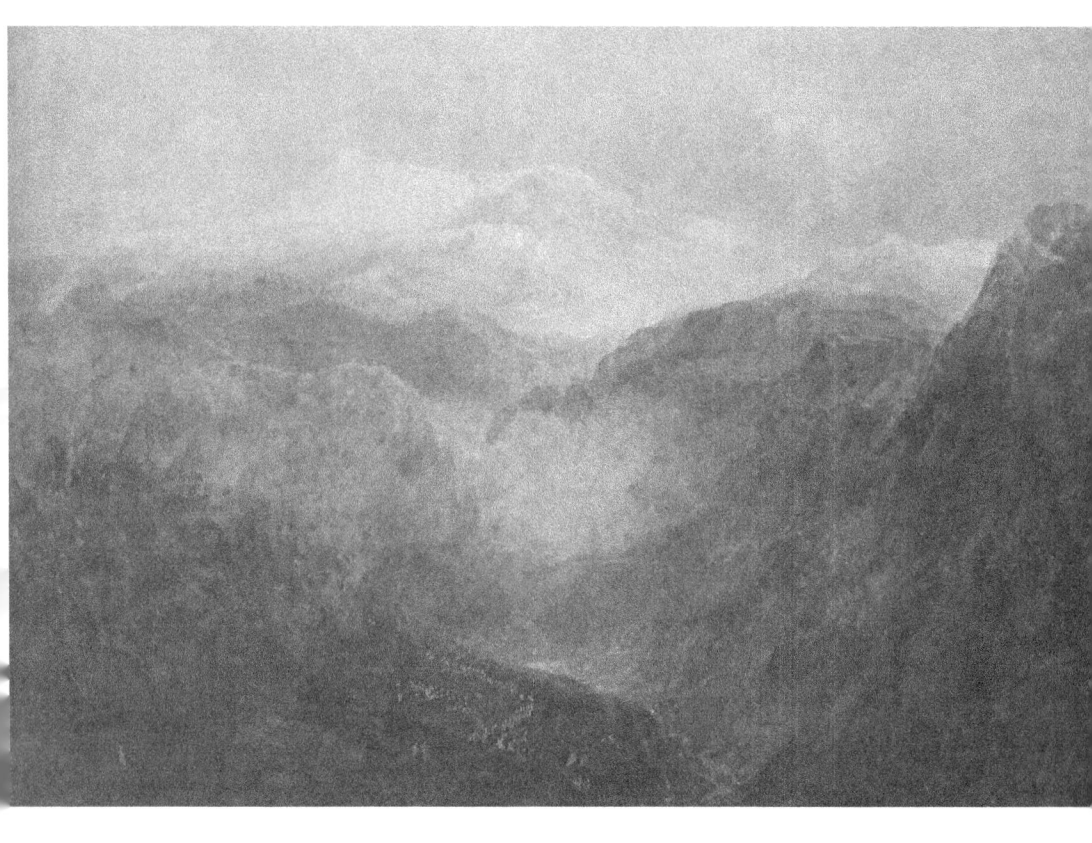

J.M.W. Turner, A Scene In the Welsh Mountains, 1799, Clore Gallery

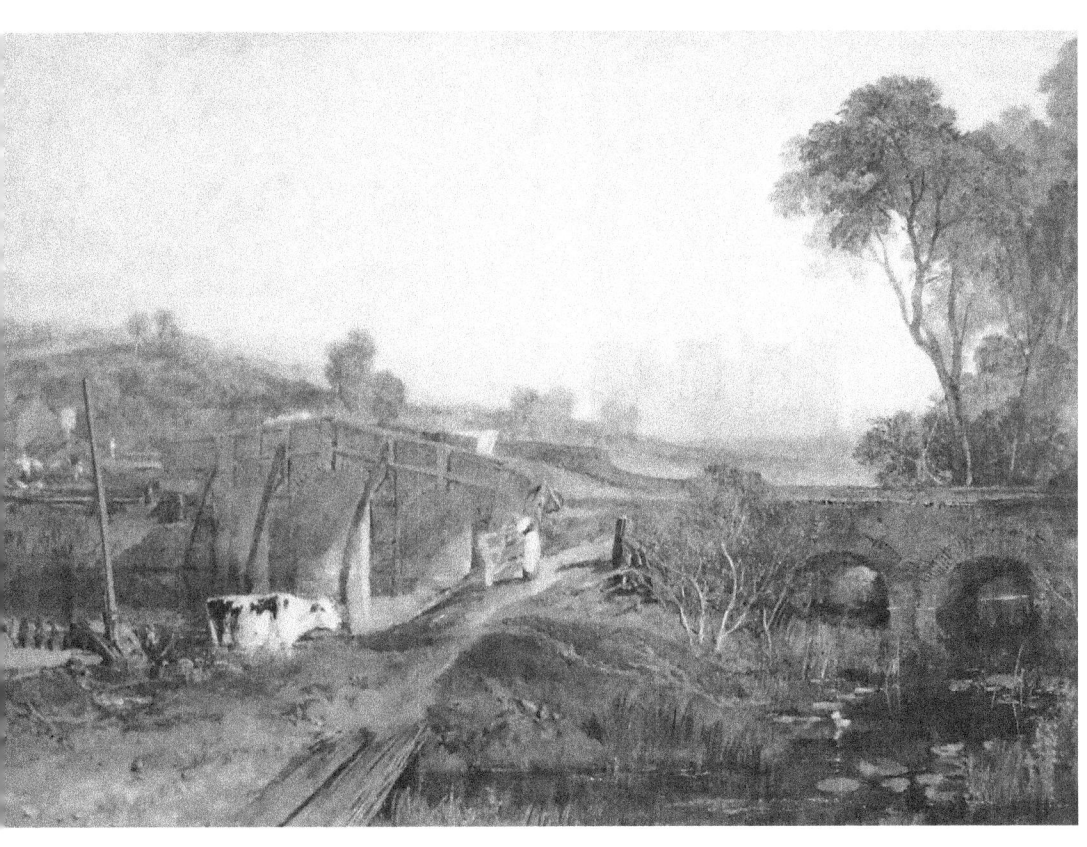

J.M.W. Turner, Bodiham Castle, c. 1816

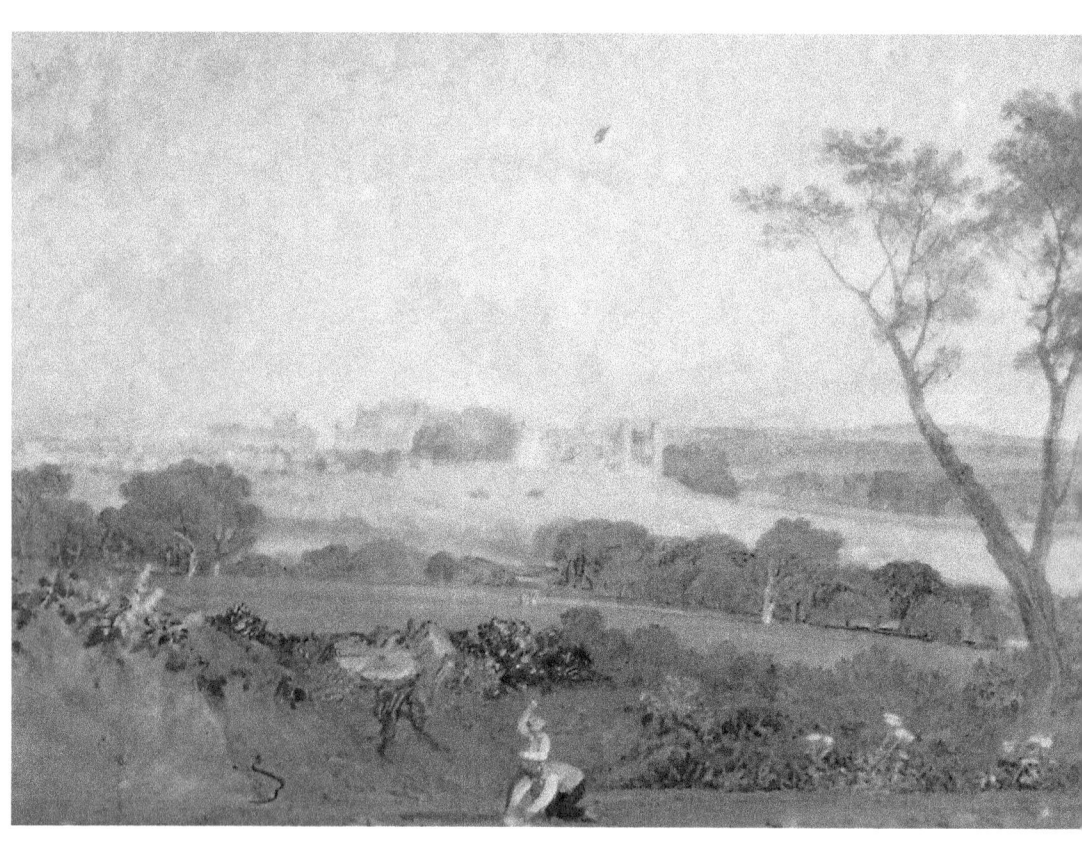

J.M.W. Turner, Battle Abbey, 1810

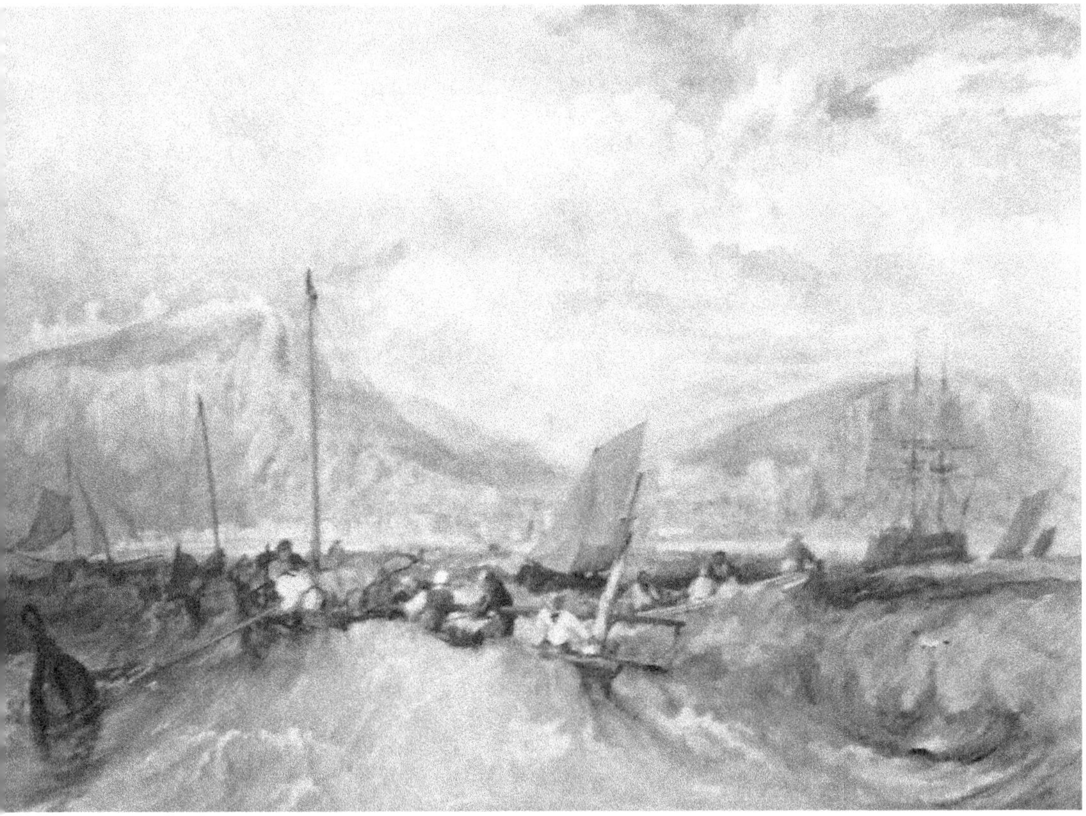

J.M.W. Turner, Hastings (above). Whitstable (below).

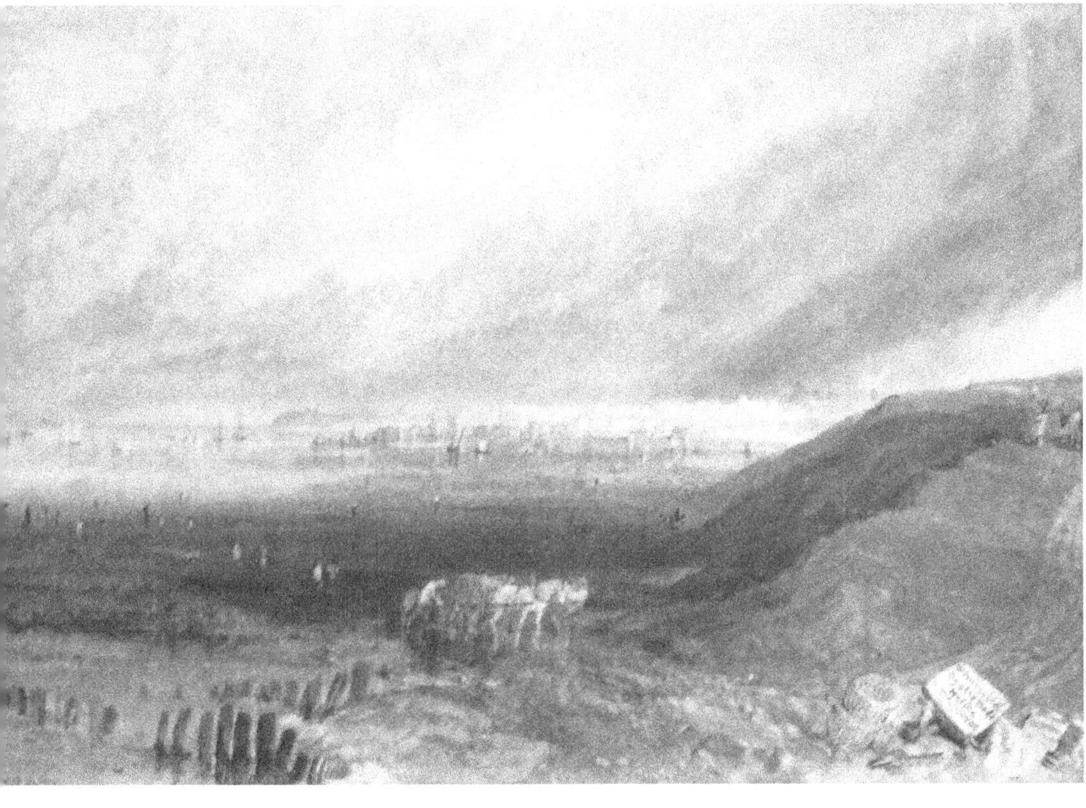

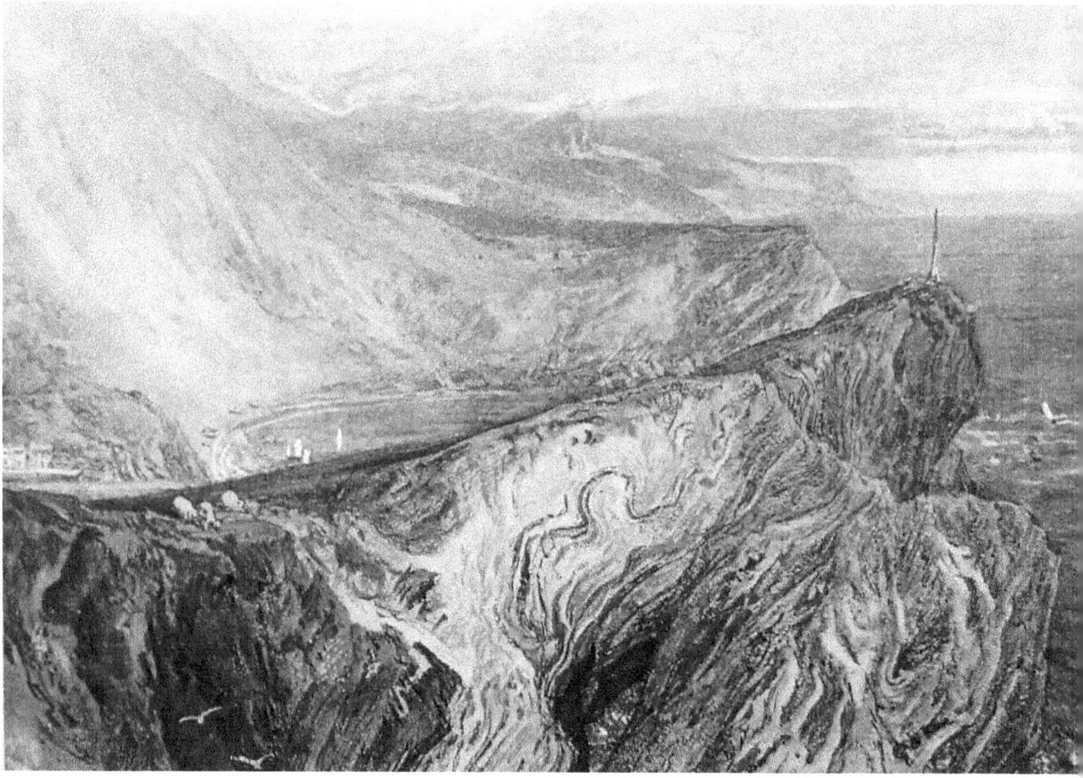

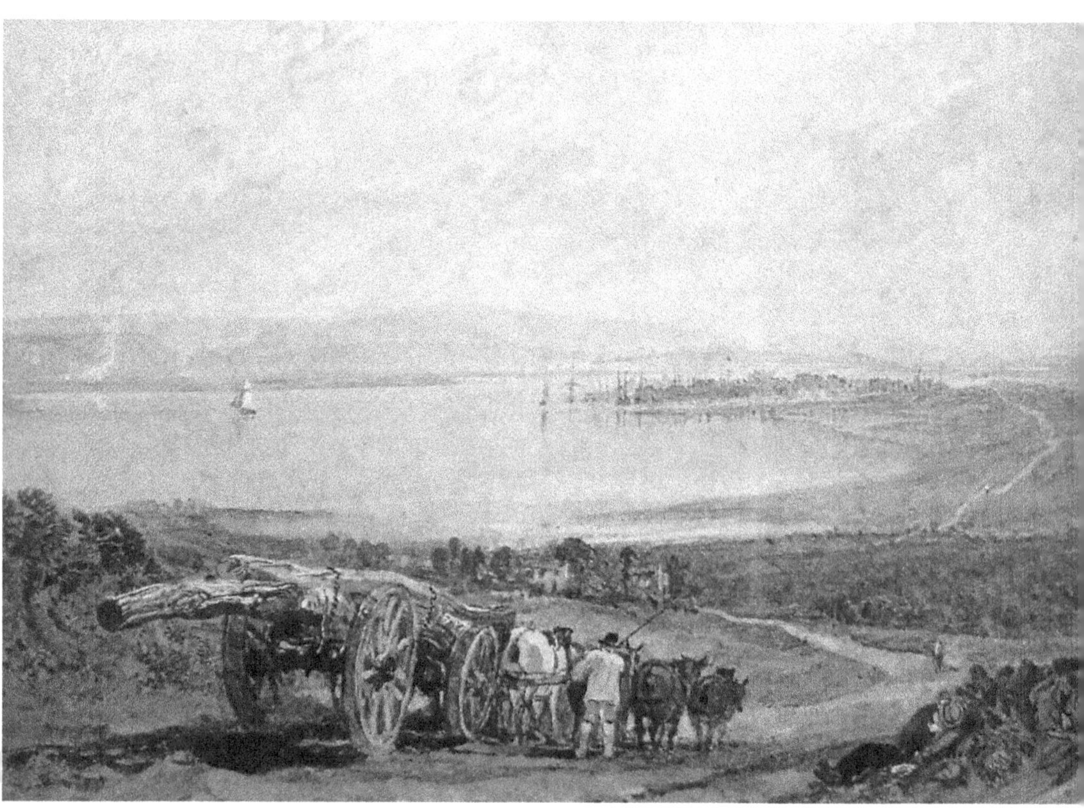

J.M.W. Turner, Poole, Dorset, c. 1811 (bottom). Lulworth Cove, Dorset, c. 1811 (top).

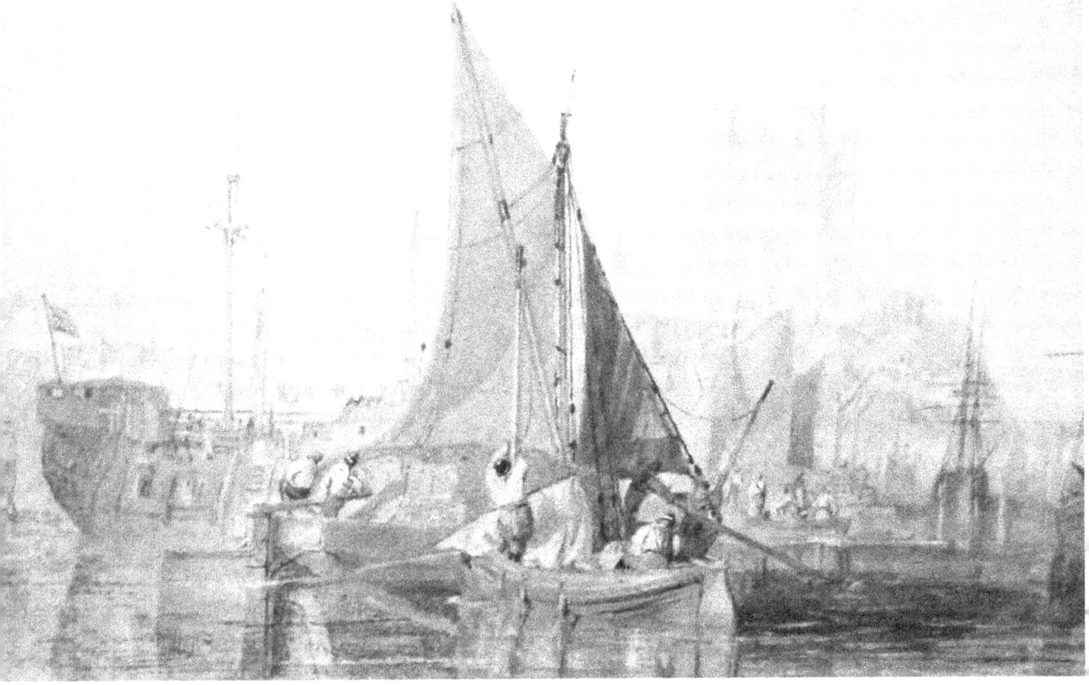

J.M.W. Turner, Rochester, On the River Medway, British Museum (above).
Stangate Creek, River Medway (below).

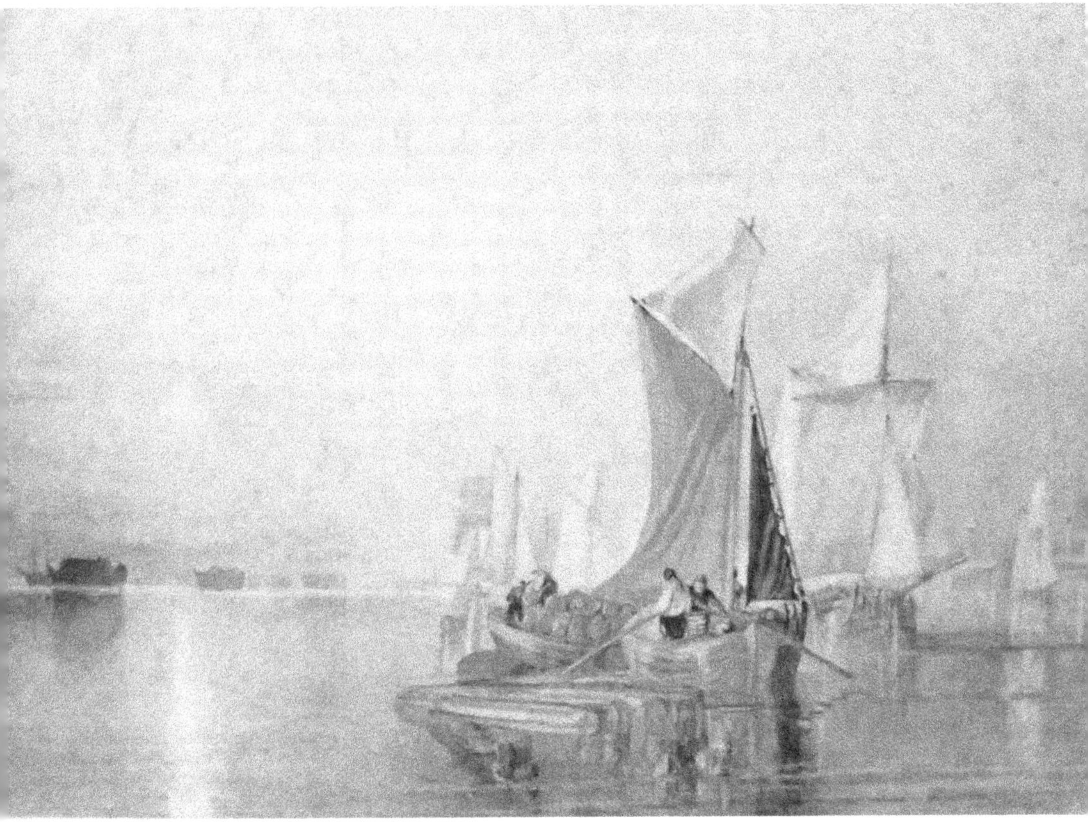

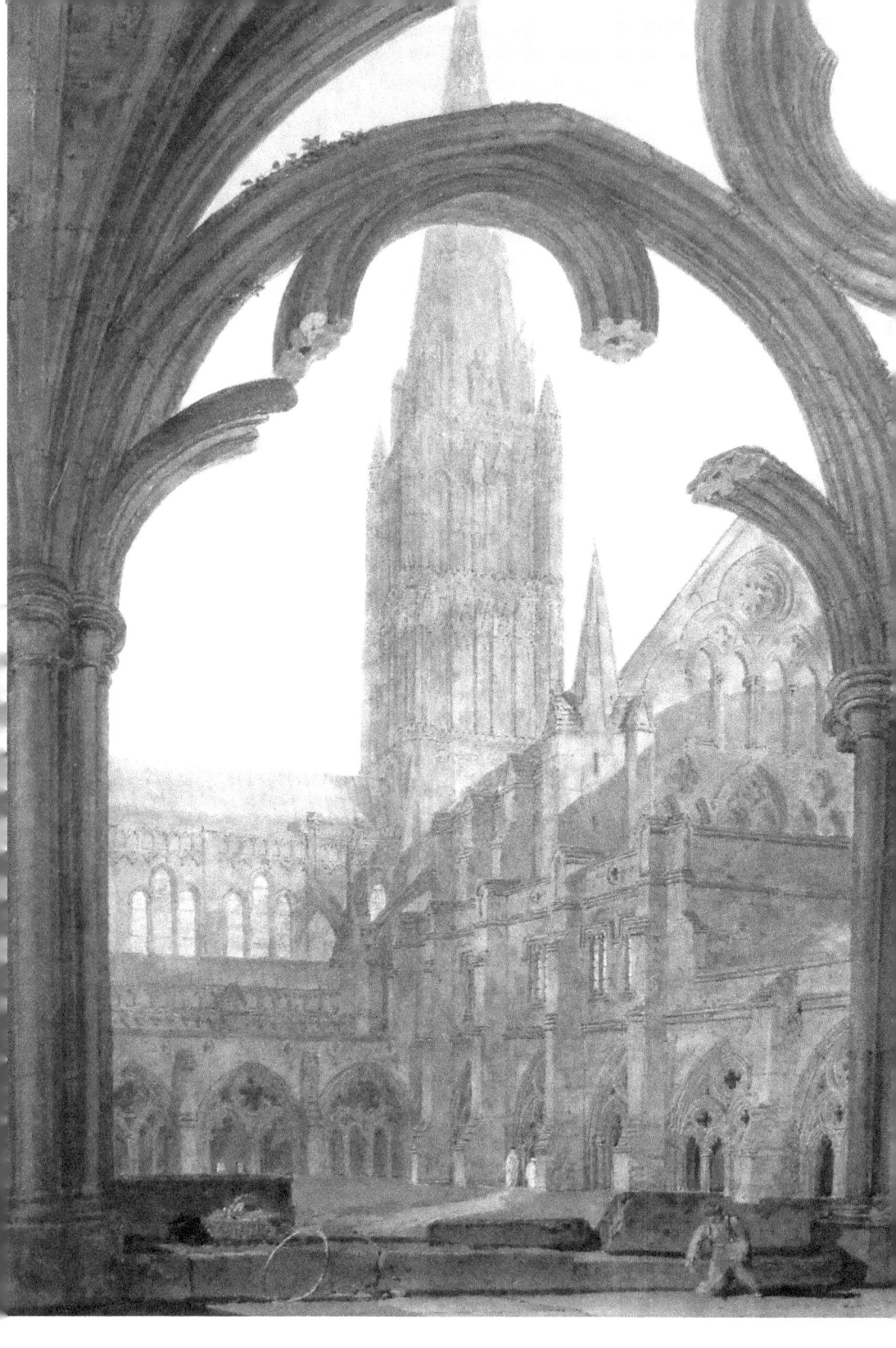

J.M.W. Turner, Salisbury Cathedral, 1802, V & A Museum, London

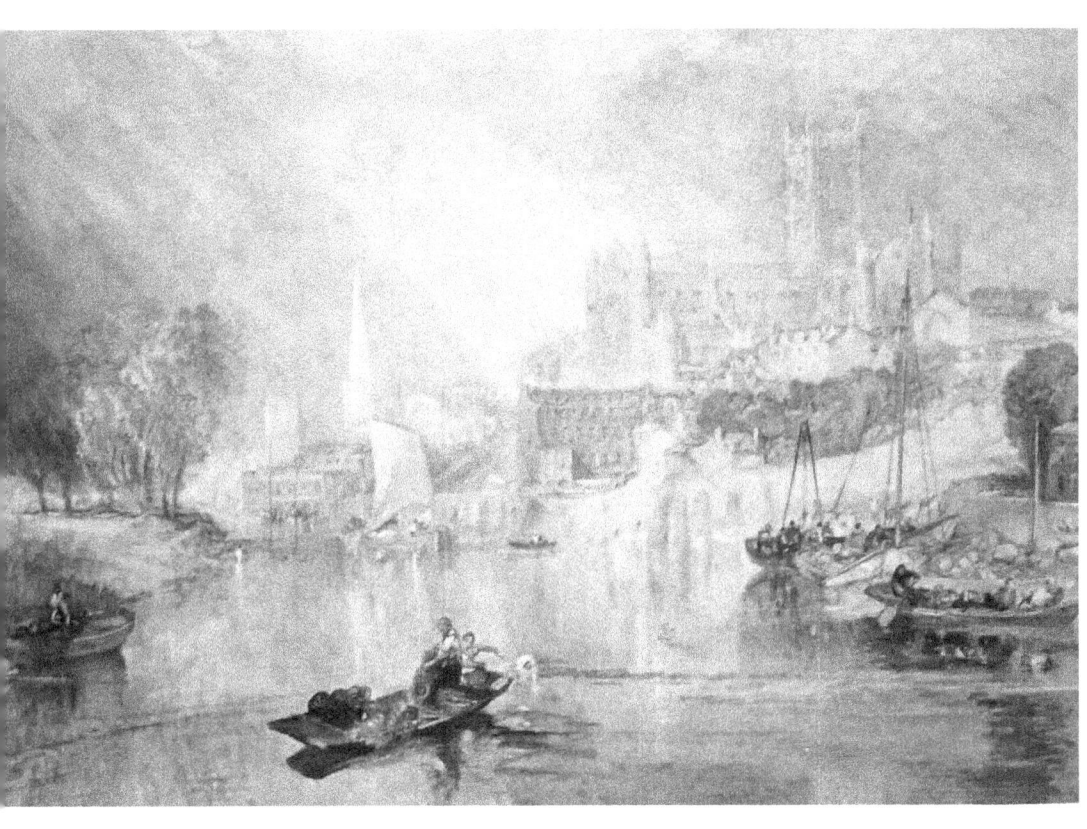

J.M.W. Turner, Worcester Cathedral, Clore Gallery

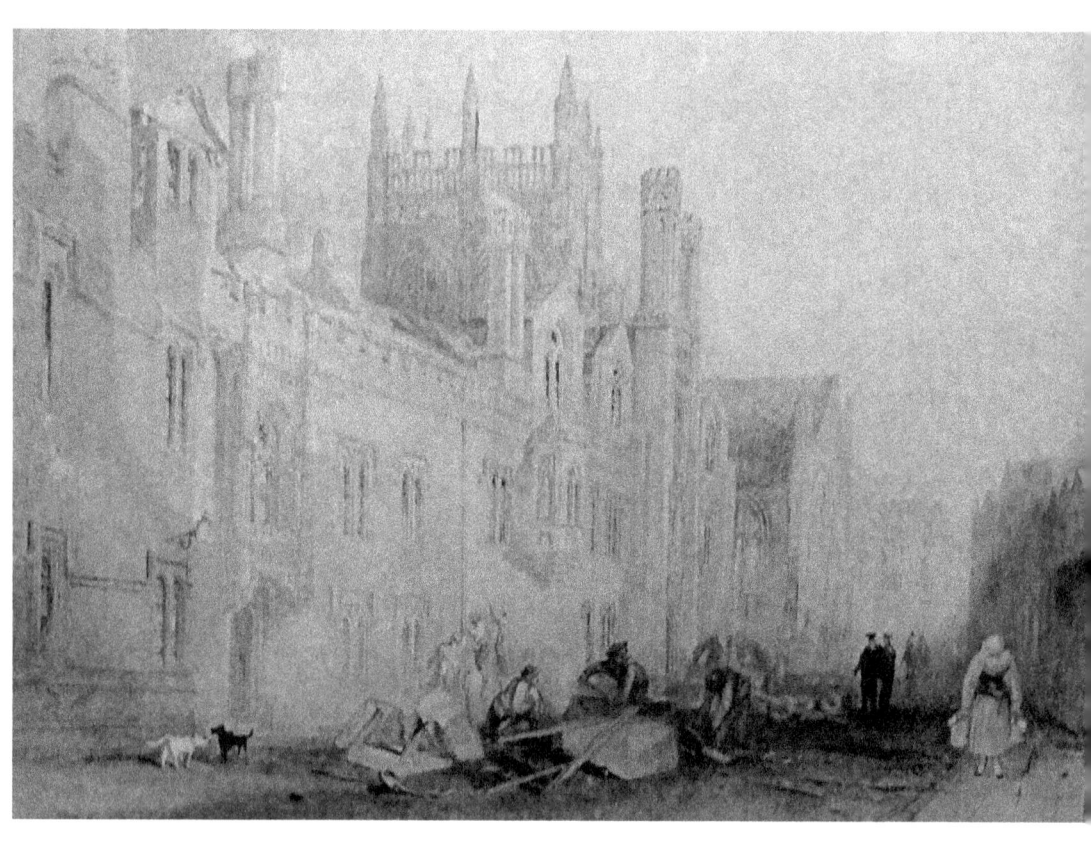

J.M.W. Turner, Merton College, Clore Gallery, London

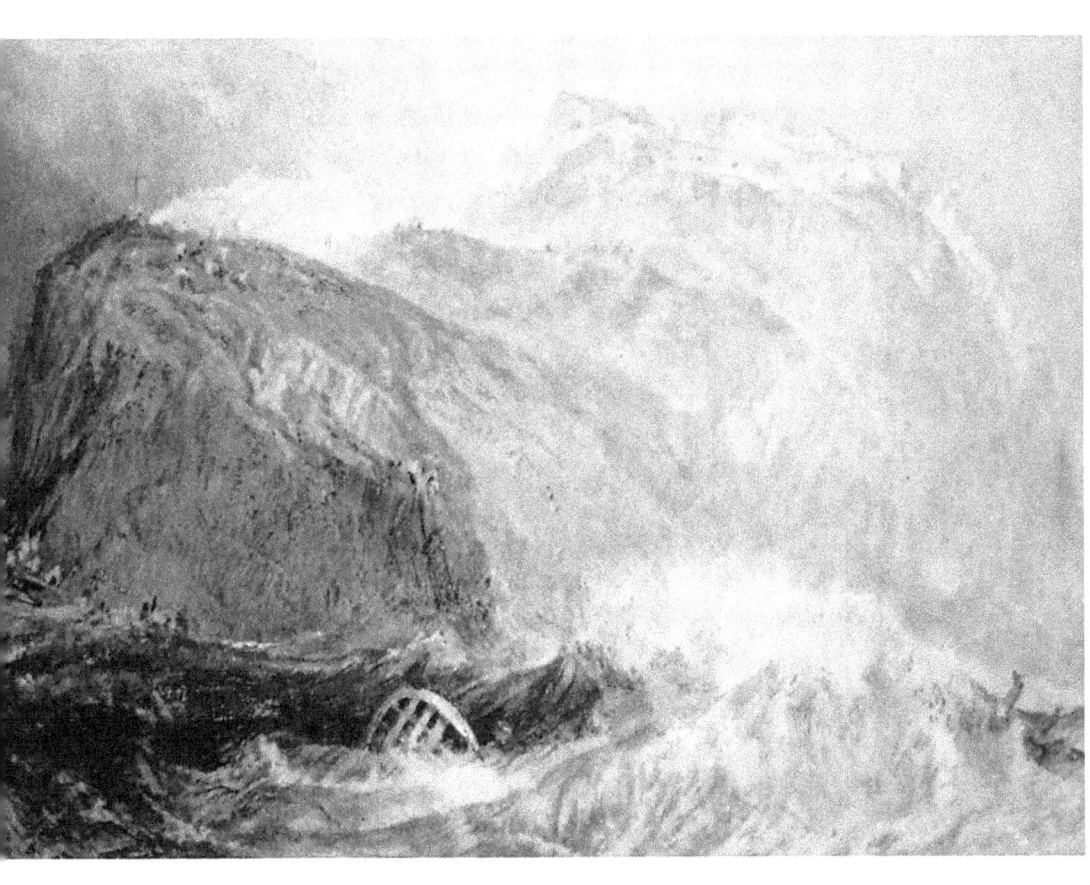

J.M.W. Turner, Tintagel Castle, 1815, Boston

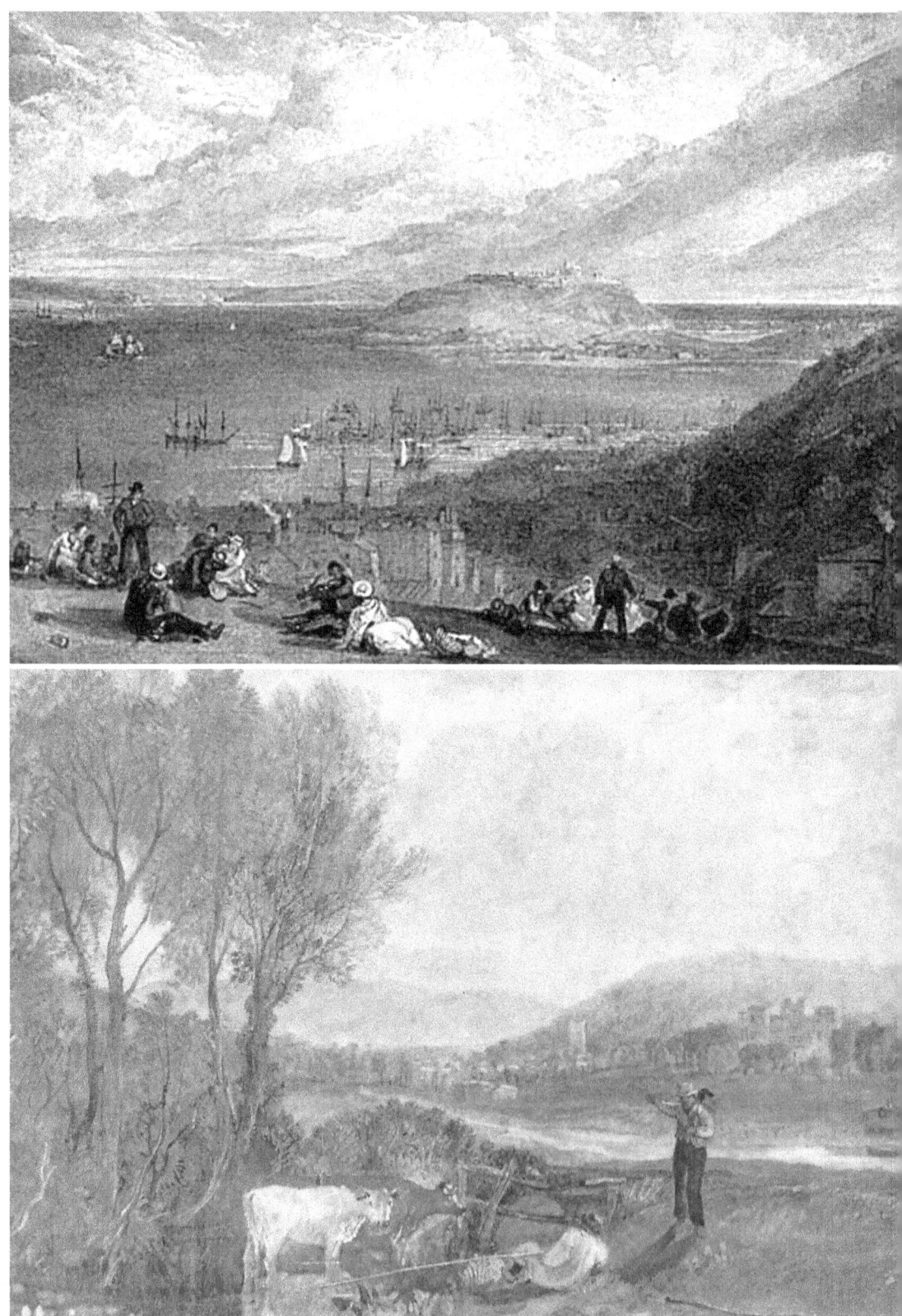

J.M.W.Turner, Falmouth Harbour, c. 1812-13 (top).
Lulworth Castle (above).

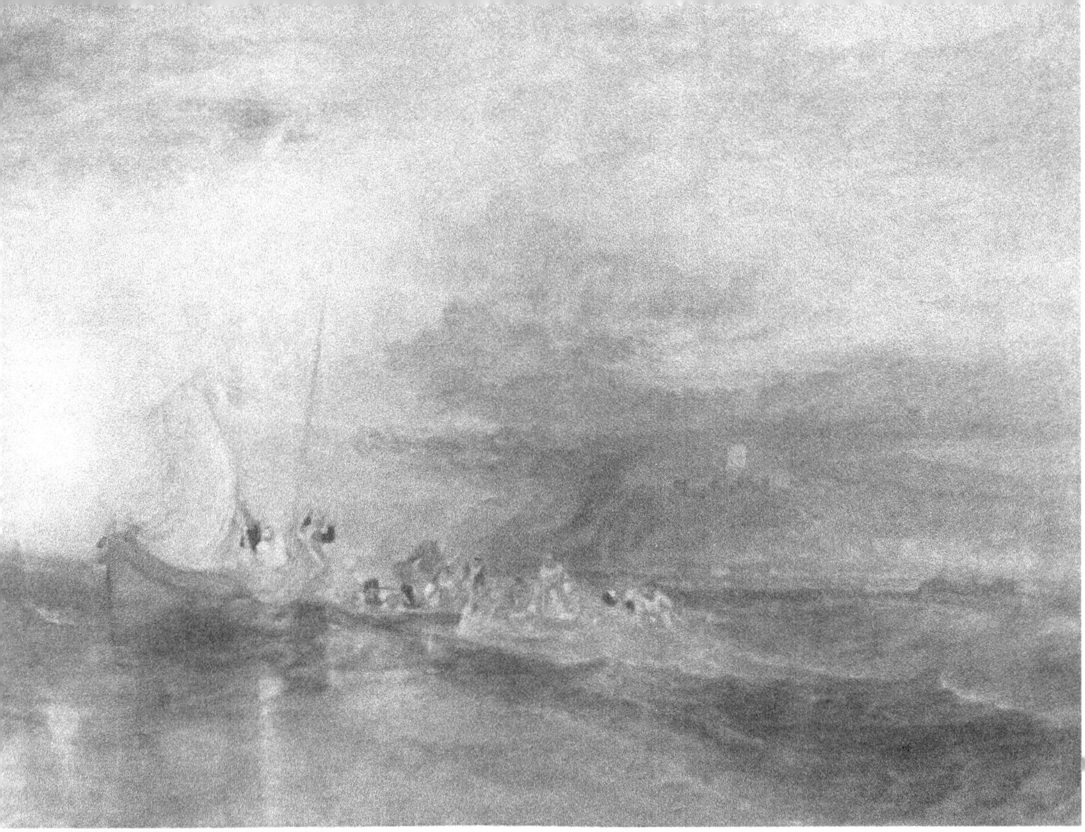

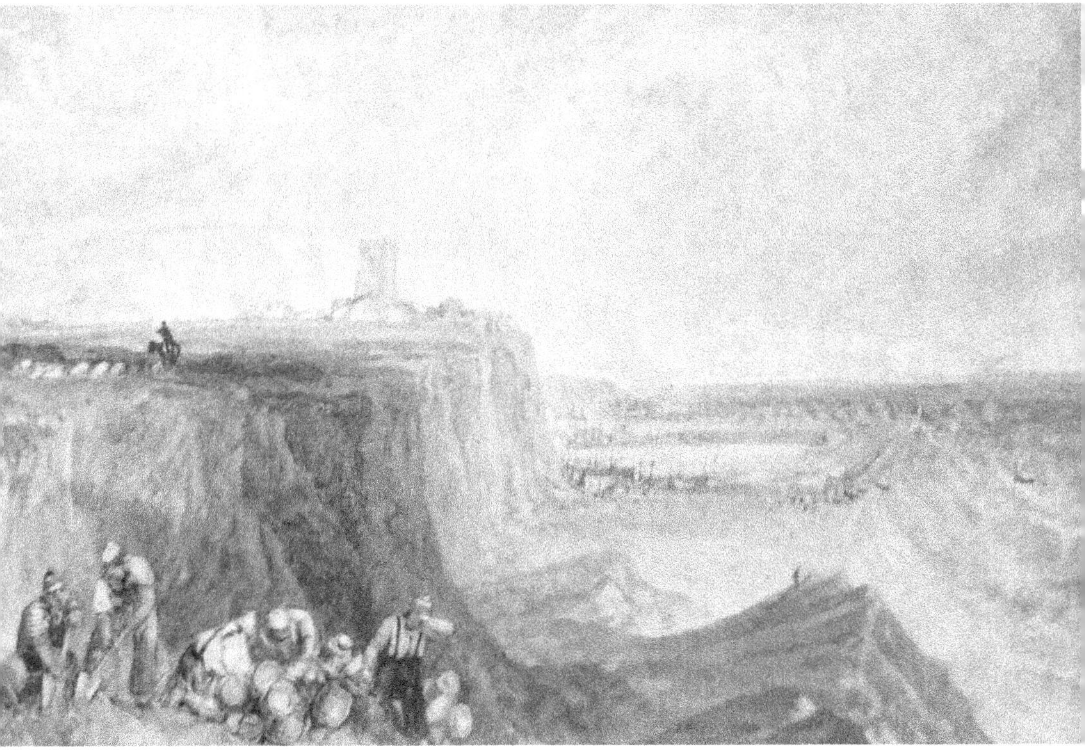

J.M.W. Turner, two views of Folkestone (top: 1822-24).

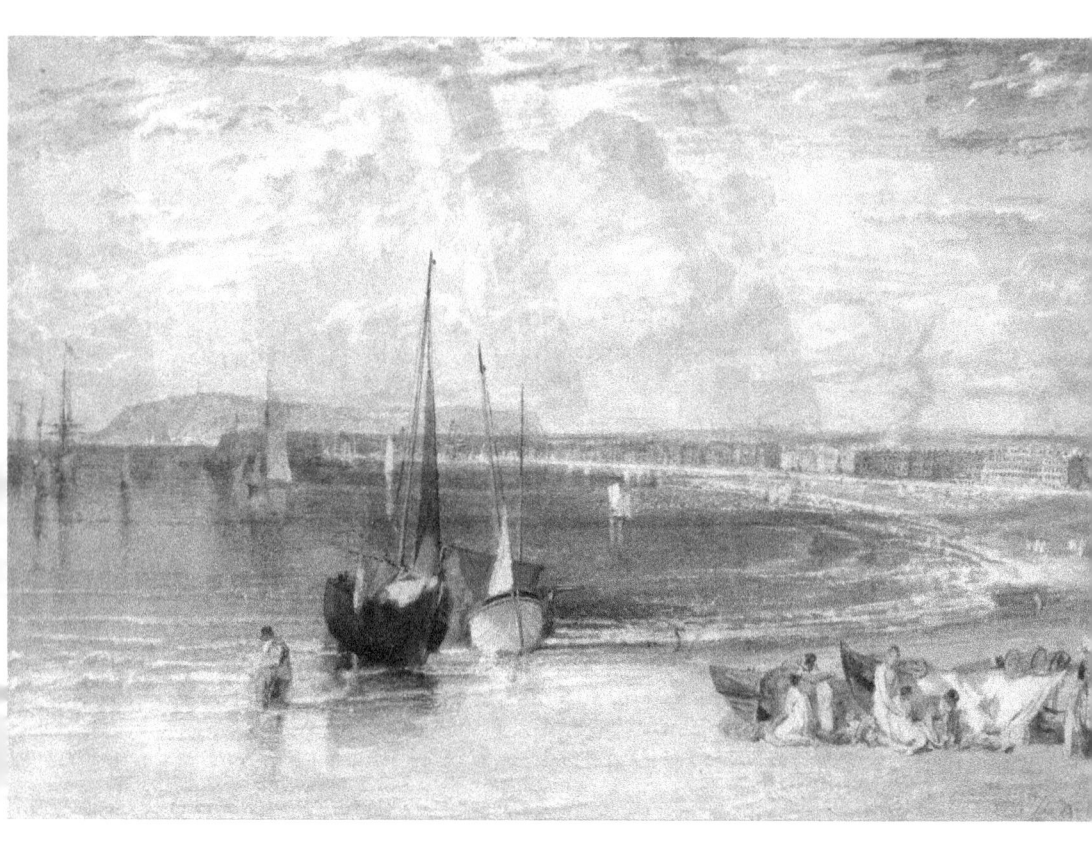

J.M.W. Turner, Weymouth, c. 1811, Yale

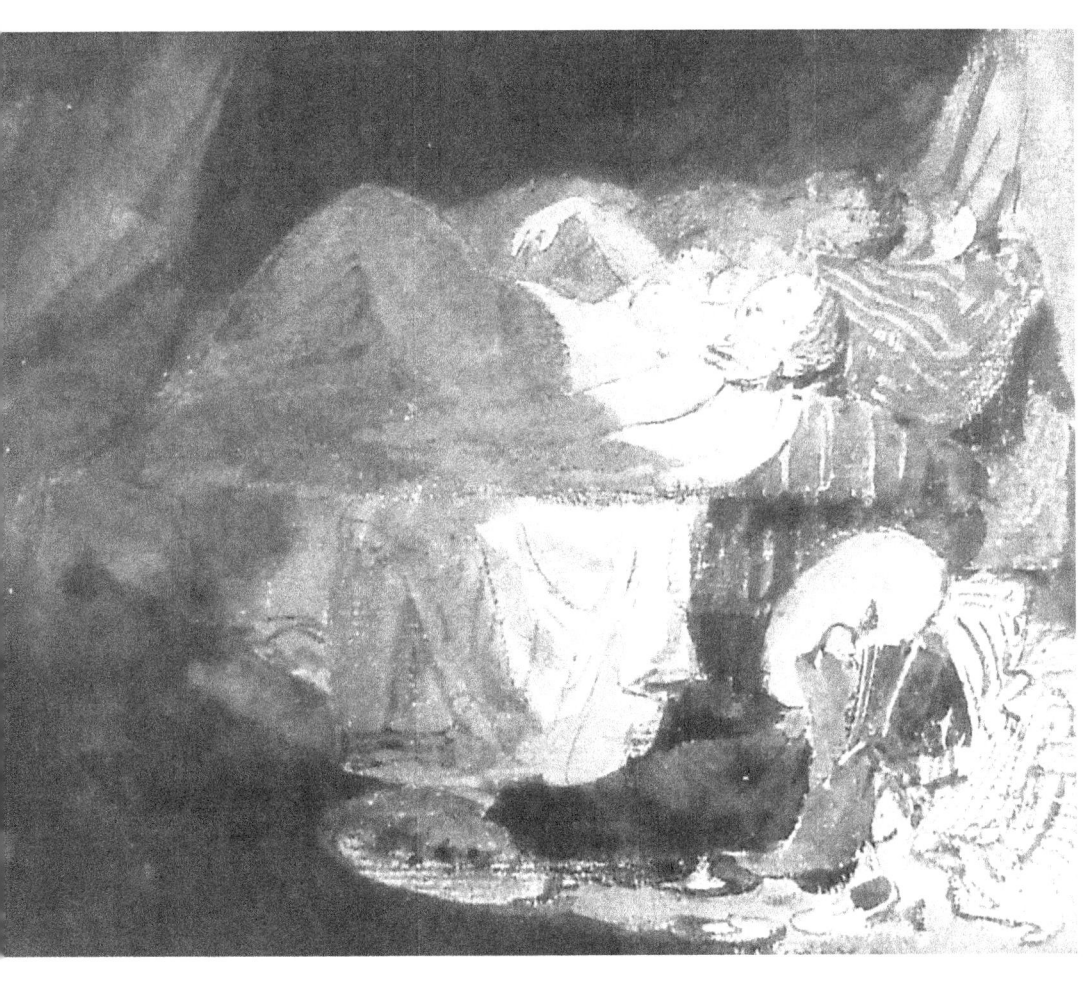

J.M.W. Turner, Two Women in Bed, 1802, Clore Gallery

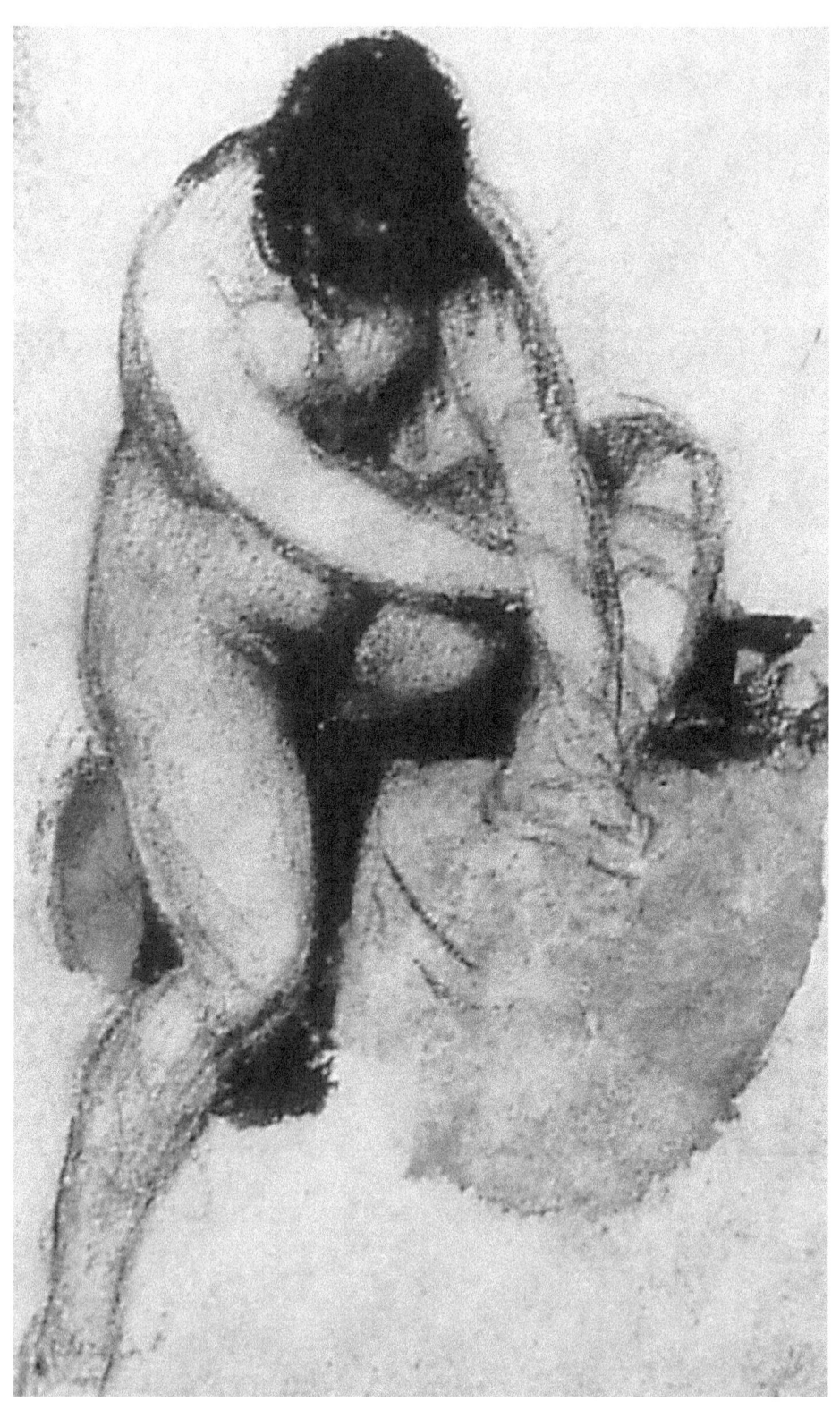

J.M.W. Turner, Seated Nude, 1904, Clore Gallery

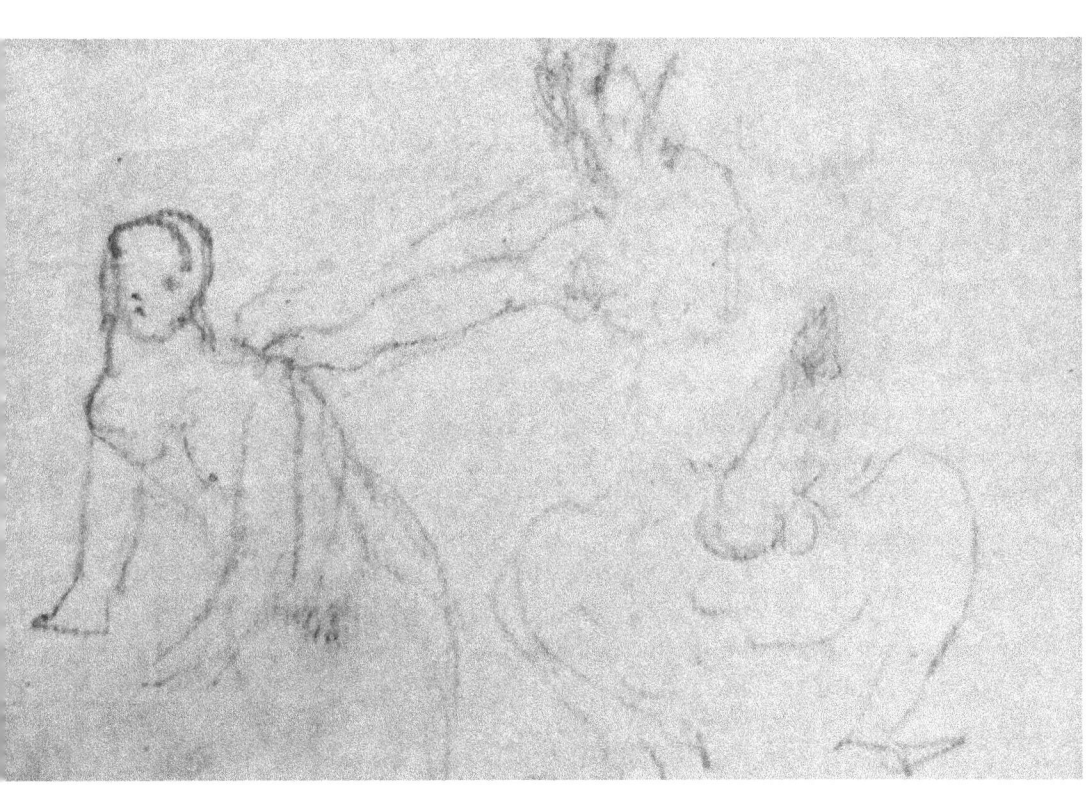

J.M.W. Turner, Nymph and Satyr, 1824

LETTER III

HIS ART: THE FURNACE DOORS OPEN

There is a small, neglected room in the National Gallery where certain beginnings and failures in art are entombed. If you were to stroll into that sepulchre on a dark day, I fear you would exclaim that "Buttermere Lake" is bright compared with those other early Turners "Morning on Coniston Fells" and "Moonlight: a Study at Millbank." Even on early March afternoons, when the sun strikes through the tall windows and falls upon "Moonlight at Millbank," little is visible on the small, sooty canvas except the full moon, looking like a discoloured white wafer stuck upon the dim sky. Turner developed slowly. This veritable nocturne, and the pictures that followed it shows how slow and difficult was his mastery of oil as a medium.

In the early nineteenth century Claude, the Poussins, Salvator Rosa, and Cuyp were the idols of landscape art, which was still regarded as a sort of interloper in the realm swayed by religious and mythological pictures, portraits, genre works, and "Dutch drolleries." The academic pioneers in landscape had imposed themselves upon Nature and upon the English gentry who were the patrons of art. Landscape might be classically beautiful according to Claude, classically sublime according to Salvator, homely and mildly sunny according to Cuyp, conventionally maritime according to Vandevelde. Turner as a youth was not the man to break tradition. The cunning tradesman in him preferred the well-beaten path. It was his destiny to compete against the popular idols in turn, to sweep past them to Nature herself, and so onwards and upwards to the sun, the source of all light and colour. "Looked on the sun with hope" is one of the few simple and suggestive lines in his "Fallacies of Hope."

Averse in his beginnings, like Velazquez, to experimentalising, he was content to bide his time, to plough the furrows of other men, with the indwelling determination to plough them better. He admired with generosity; he never depreciated. "Vandevelde made me a painter," he said, years later, and of a golden-brown Cuyp he exclaimed, "I would give a thousand pounds to have painted that."

If ever, exiled student, we visit the National Gallery together on the Turner quest, I shall take you first to that room where, from the grave, he challenges Claude of Lorraine. Turner bequeathed "The Sun Rising in a Mist," painted when he was thirty-two, and "Dido Building Carthage," painted when he was forty, to the nation, on condition that they should hang for ever "between the two pictures painted by Claude, the 'Seaport' and the 'Mill,'" There you have a glimpse into the mind of Turner, his fine envy of others, his confidence in his own power. A Frenchman, M. Viardot, incensed at the idea that any one should approach the throne of the Lorrainer, suggests that such o'ervaulting pride was a proof of Turner's insanity. I will not answer such foolishness, but British candour compels me to say that I do not think Claude suffers by the comparison. Turner became great when he became himself, not when he was trying to outvie others – Titian, Morland, Gainsborough, Crome – to name but four. In the year that he painted "The Sun Rising in a Mist" he was trying in his "Country Blacksmith" to trip Wilkie, and in "The Sun Rising in a Mist," as Mr. Wyllie shows, the figures are taken almost exactly from Teniers, and the snub-nosed, high-pooped ships from Vandevelde. His time was not yet. He was learning furiously, brooding upon and correlating his impressions of Nature, storing them for future use, shredding the permanent from the trivial. I think of him on that tossing trip to Bur Island in a half-decked boat with Cyrus Redding, silently watching the sea, absorbed in contemplation, climbing to the summit of the island in a hurricane of wind, where he "seemed writing rather than drawing." Not yet could he say to a companion, looking at a black cow against the sun, "It's purple, not black as it is painted"; not yet had the sun begun to flood his drawings; not yet were the "brown tree school" angry because forms lost their details in the blinding light of his pictures. But in "Dido building Carthage," painted in 1815, the same year as the popular "Crossing the Brook," of which he thought so highly that he talked in his ironic, humorous way of being wrapped up in it as a winding-sheet, there are signs that he was feeling the fascination of colour.

Some day you will stand at the entrance of the great Turner Room in the National Gallery and rest your eyes on the six huge dark pictures on the left wall. The dull and uninspiring "Waterloo" is later than the others; but to me it is just as unattractive as its companions – as I think it will be, light lover, to you. "The Tenth Plague" and "The Deluge" I never look at except when I wish to be reminded that from the chrysalis rises the butterfly, from the black furnace the loveliness of the flame. The "Death of Nelson" is dark and decorative, "Calais Pier" and "The Shipwreck" are dark and tremendous. "Nobody is wet," said Ruskin, and nobody feels that he is looking on the real Calais, or on a real shipwreck, yet what power they have. These funereal wild waves were made in Harley Street; light, to the slow-developing Turner, was still a studio convention. But nobody else could have made those seas. They are by Turner, but not by the true Turner, who strove through the veiled sun to the source of light itself.

In "Crossing the Brook," which faces the entrance doorway, painted when he was forty, Turner has marched onward. The gates have opened to the far horizon, and he now gives us the Turnerian fifty miles or so of country outstretching to infinity on a few feet of canvas. If you were with me, I would whisper in your ear my division of "Crossing the Brook" into pleasing and unpleasing passages – the pleasing being the fleecy clouds in the blue sky, the faint miles of Devonshire, the wooded hills rising from the river, and the bridge that spans the water: the unpleasing passages are the worried foreground, the ugly rocks, the figures, and the black mouth of the tunnel. Yet it is a picture of which one becomes fond. Who can but be entranced by the distance, Turner's sign mark, the open gate that lures us away from the troubled foreground of the world.

I turn from the sanity of "Crossing the Brook" to the right wall, and straightway I am elated, it is always so, at the sight of one of the magnificent dreams that the old Wizard forced oil paint and brushes to portray. In the centre of the wall hangs "Ulysses and Polyphemus."

The furnace doors are open, from them stream a fury of glow, and in the fire are the dazzling shapes of Turnerian romance.

LETTER IV

THE FLAME ASCENDS

When we visit the National Gallery I will place you with your back to the dark "Calais Pier" and "Shipwreck" wall, and waving my hand across to that glorious trio, the "Ulysses," the "Bay of Baiæ," and the "Carthage," I will say but one word – "Turner!"

Here indeed is the magician weaving his spells, breaking the laws of light and shade, toying with history, caring nothing so long as he can picture the dreams of the pomp and beauty of the world of imagination that dazzled a sullen man, pottering about in a dingy London studio. "Ulysses deriding Polyphemus" has been called operatic and melodramatic; it has been remarked that the galley of Ulysses, far from the influence of the sun, is in full light, and that the dark shadows thrown by the stone-pines in the "Bay of Baiæ" are unnatural. Turner needed those deep blacks in the foreground; he wanted the galley of Ulysses to be in the light: so the old rascal forced truth to suit his vision. His success is his expiation. He never copied Nature or followed history. His way was to use Nature and history to suit his conception, the right way for a genius; but not for Brown, Smith, and Jones. Anachronisms abound in his works; he elongated steeples, rebuilt towers and towns, changed the courses of rivers (he in paint, as Leonardo with the pencil); but he caught the spirit of place. To me the "Ulysses deriding Polyphemus" is the very heart of romance. Unlike life, yes; all the best things are unlike life. I withdraw my remark that there is not a figure in a picture by Turner which I would not rather have erased, withdraw it in favour of the vast, impotent Polyphemus writhing on the cliff. When Turner painted the figures of gods and goddesses in the likeness of men and women he was bored; when he painted a giant monster like this Polyphemus his imagination inspired him. Asked where he found his subject, he invented two silly lines of doggerel and said they came from Tom Dibdin. His lonely visions were not for the chatter of a dinner party. They may be tracked in that little red book found by Thornbury in his studio, where, amid notes about chemistry, memoranda as to colours, and prophylactics against the Maltese plague, are certain scraps of verse, something about, "Anna's kiss," "a look back," "a toilsome dream," "human joy, ecstasy, and hope."

Here I pause to ask myself how I can possibly give you, who have never seen it, an idea of the Turner room at the National Gallery. I close my eyes and visualise the route. I ascend the stairs, and am detained by two Turners that have, against his will, overflowed into an outer room – the beautiful heat-hazy Abingdon, and distant London, seen from Greenwich. Almost reluctantly I walk into the large gallery, and pass from the glorious sunrise in Ulysses to the glorious sunset in "The Fighting Téméraire," painted just ten years later. Claude and the others have been left far behind. Here is Turner the visionary, alone with the sun and the sea, untroubled by the necessity of painting the puny figure of man, but glorying in the symbols of man's power, the new tug dragging the stately old battleship to her last berth, a theme near to his heart – the end of a period in man's history flickering out in the ageless glory of Nature.

Pages, chapters, have been written about the untruth of this picture. "His light and shade," says Mr. Wyllie, "is very seldom correct. His tones are almost always wrong. The place where the sun is setting in the 'Téméraire' is the darkest part of the picture." But what does it matter? This is his vision, of the absolute end of man's work in this daily death of Nature. Who would have one inch changed? About this, as about almost all the pictures, there is a story. The Téméraire "killed" a portrait by Geddes hanging above it, whereupon Geddes began to lay in a vivid Turkey carpet on his canvas. "Ho! ho!" cried Turner, who loved a fight; and the unfortunate Geddes watched him loading on orange, scarlet, and yellow with his palette knife.

I close my eyes to the splendour of the "Téméraire" and see "The Burial of Wilkie," a silvery blue sky and sea shimmering with delicate reflections, the mourning, black-sailed vessel severed by the flare of the torches, their brilliancy and the black of the sails forming vast tracks of light and gloom on the water. On Varnishing Day Stanfield urged that the sails were untrue. Turner grunted – "Wish I had any colour to make 'em blacker."

Then I see the "Snowstorm – Steamboat off a Harbour's Mouth making Signals in Shallow Water and going by the lead," which *Punch* called "A Typhoon bursting in a Simoon over the Whirlpool of Maelstrom, Norway, with a ship on fire, an eclipse, and the effect of a lunar rainbow." Turner is now sixty-seven. He is prepared to push paint to its ultimate limit so that he can achieve the impossible. To study the effect of this hubbub of snowstorm and gale he put to sea in the tempest, and made the sailors lash him to the mast for four hours. It was the hostile reception of this picture following the attacks on others in previous years, the jeers of *Punch*, the shafts of *Blackwood*, that inspired Ruskin to compose "Modern Painters." The first volume was published the following year, 1843, but that colossal work had its beginnings in a letter Ruskin wrote in 1836 defending Turner's picture of Venice called "Juliet and her Nurse."

Turner was famous long before "Modern Painters" was published, and although that pæan of appreciation has carried his fame to the ends of the English-speaking world, the riot of its praise has tipped the pens of some critics with gall. The "Slave

Ship" exalted so eloquently by Ruskin, and now in Boston, was described by George Inness, the American artist, as "the most infernal piece of clap-trap ever painted."

The aged Turner suffered from the criticisms of the "Snowstorm." Ruskin tells how he heard the old man one evening muttering to himself "Soapsuds and Whitewash." On the "Graduate of Oxford" attempting to soothe him, he burst out – "What would they have? I wonder what they think the sea's like? I wish they'd been in it!"

Beneath the "Snowstorm" at the National Gallery hang two pictures, shining with a radiance not of the earth, "The Sun of Venice going to Sea," and "The Approach to Venice," wrecks perhaps of what they were, but still lovely, in one all the pomp of Venice, in the other all her haunting and elusive beauty. A little further along the wall in the direction of the "Ulysses" is the parent picture of Impressionism, that incomparable presentment of movement, mist, and moisture, aptly named "Rain, Steam, and Speed." The fools called this a phantom picture, complained that the locomotive has not the appearance of metal. Turner was not painting the fact of an engine; but the effect of an engine rushing through rain and mist. "My business," he once said to Cyrus Redding, "is to draw what I see: not what I know is there."

In the years 1845 and 1846, when his sense of form began to fail, but not his sense of colour, he re-saw the sea and the sun, to the exclusion of other aspects of Nature. Of the thirteen pictures painted in those two years, all but three were of Venice or of Whalers.

I wish, after our visit to the National Gallery, I could have taken you to the Old Masters Exhibition, and there bid you look at his "Mercury and Hersé," painted in 1811, when he saw with the eyes of Claude. Pleasant are the blue lakes, the distances and the veiled horizon, the faint hills and the arching sky; but they are derivative as the drawing-master trees and the wooden foreground with its score of dummy figures, its posed Mercury, its unrealised Hersé, and its architectural litter. When you had absorbed this "Mercury and Hersé" of 1811, I would have turned your gaze to the "Burning of the Houses of Parliament" of 1835, the real Turner, seeing with his own eyes the fury of burning buildings, an orgy of flames roaring up to the star-sown sky. The far end of the stone bridge, a nocturne in the palest blues and yellows, drops into the fire, half the sky is aglow, half is a night blue, and the gold and sapphire are reflected in the water, where dim boats push out from the shade into the dazzle, and thousands of figures, mere suggestions of forms, watch the two towers, molten silver, standing solitary and self-contained like Shadrach, Meshach, and Abed-nego in the flames.

It was such spade-work as the "Liber Studiorum" that enabled him to triumph in such an impossible subject as "The Burning of the Houses of Parliament." Imagine what this series of drawings meant! Claude's "Liber Veritatis," to rival which the "Liber Studiorum" was designed, was a mere record of his pictures. Turner's "Liber Studiorum" was a survey of Nature, classified under six heads, – architectural, pastoral, elegant or epic-pastoral, marine, mountainous, and historical or heroic. These divisions were suggested by "Dad." "Well, Gaffer," said Turner, "I see there will be no peace till I comply; so give me a piece of paper." He made each drawing in sepia; he etched the essential lines, and he trained a school of engravers (not without quarrelling) to engrave them.

Men have loved the "Liber." Connoisseurs, like Mr. Rawlinson, have specialised in it. I know an enthusiast who spends hours in the course of the year, smoking his pipe, gazing at (a poor impression, but his own) No. VII., "The Straw Yard," that hangs on his study-wall against a reproduction of Girtin's "White House at Chelsea," and he wonders which he would save first if the house caught fire. I have been a quarter of an hour late for an appointment through returning twice to a certain house to enjoy again Mr. Frank Short's engravings of two of the unpublished drawings – the "Crowhurst" and the "Stonehenge." But I never knew what the "Liber" really was until I saw Mr. Rawlinson's collection, the depth and velvety richness of a very early state of the "Raglan Castle," and the large and still simplicity of the "Junction of Severn and Wye." Some day it may be your privilege to see them; but first we will descend to the ground floor of the National Gallery and please ourselves by making a choice among the seventy and more sepia drawings for the "Liber" that hang on the wall of the first room.

But I doubt if you will have patience to go through all, for around, and in little rooms beyond, are the water-colours.

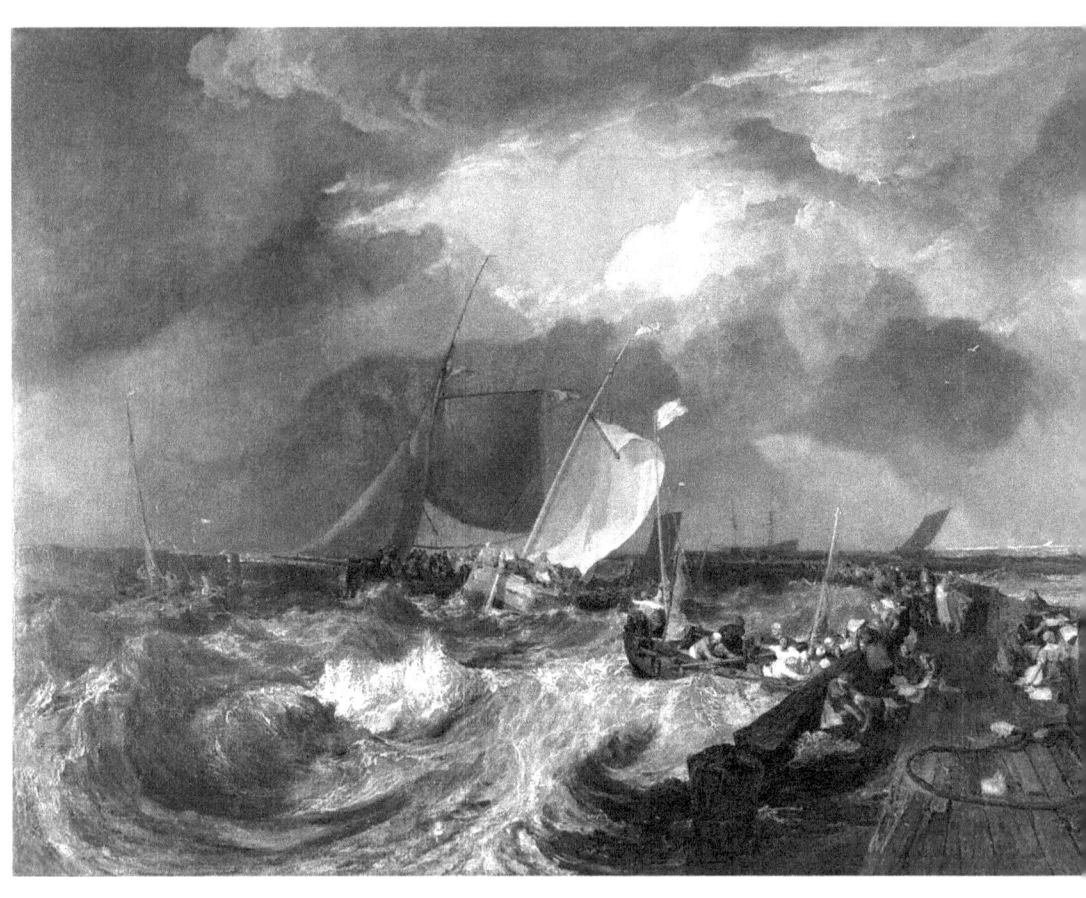

J.M.W. Turner, Calais Pier, 1803, London

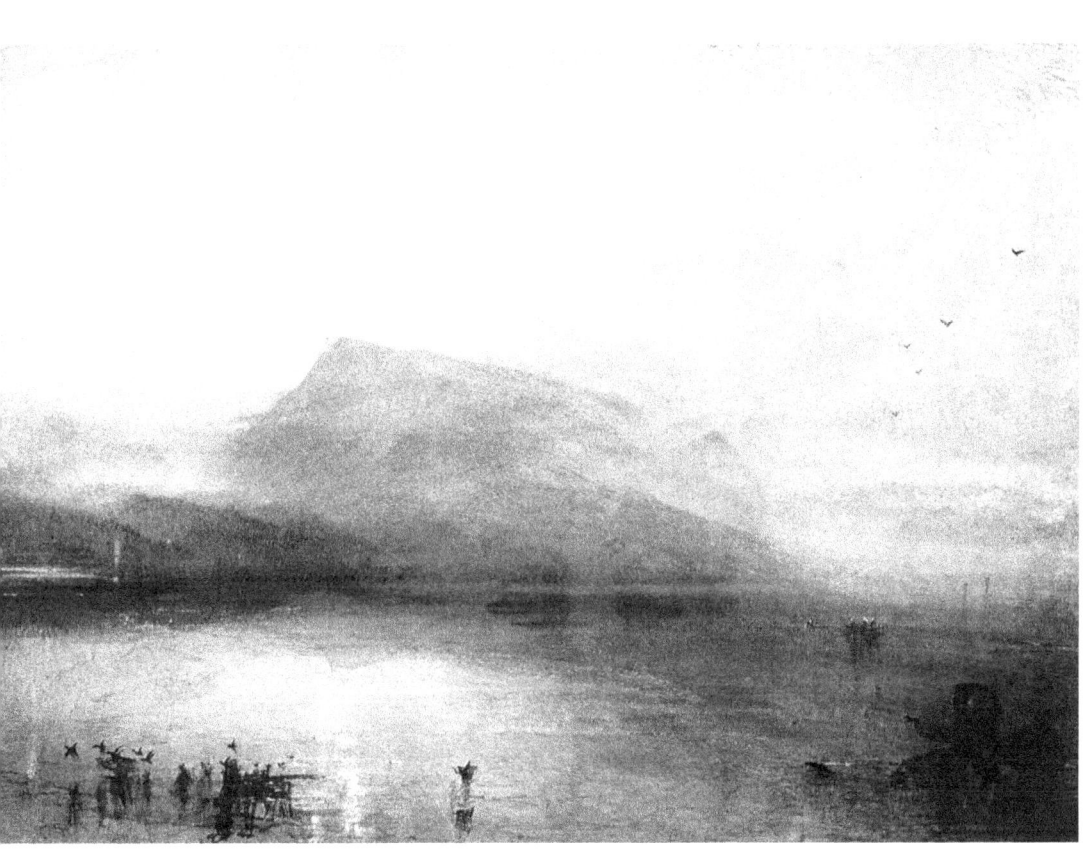

J.M.W. Turner, The Blue Rigi, Lake of Lucerne, Sunrise,
1842, Clore Gallery, London

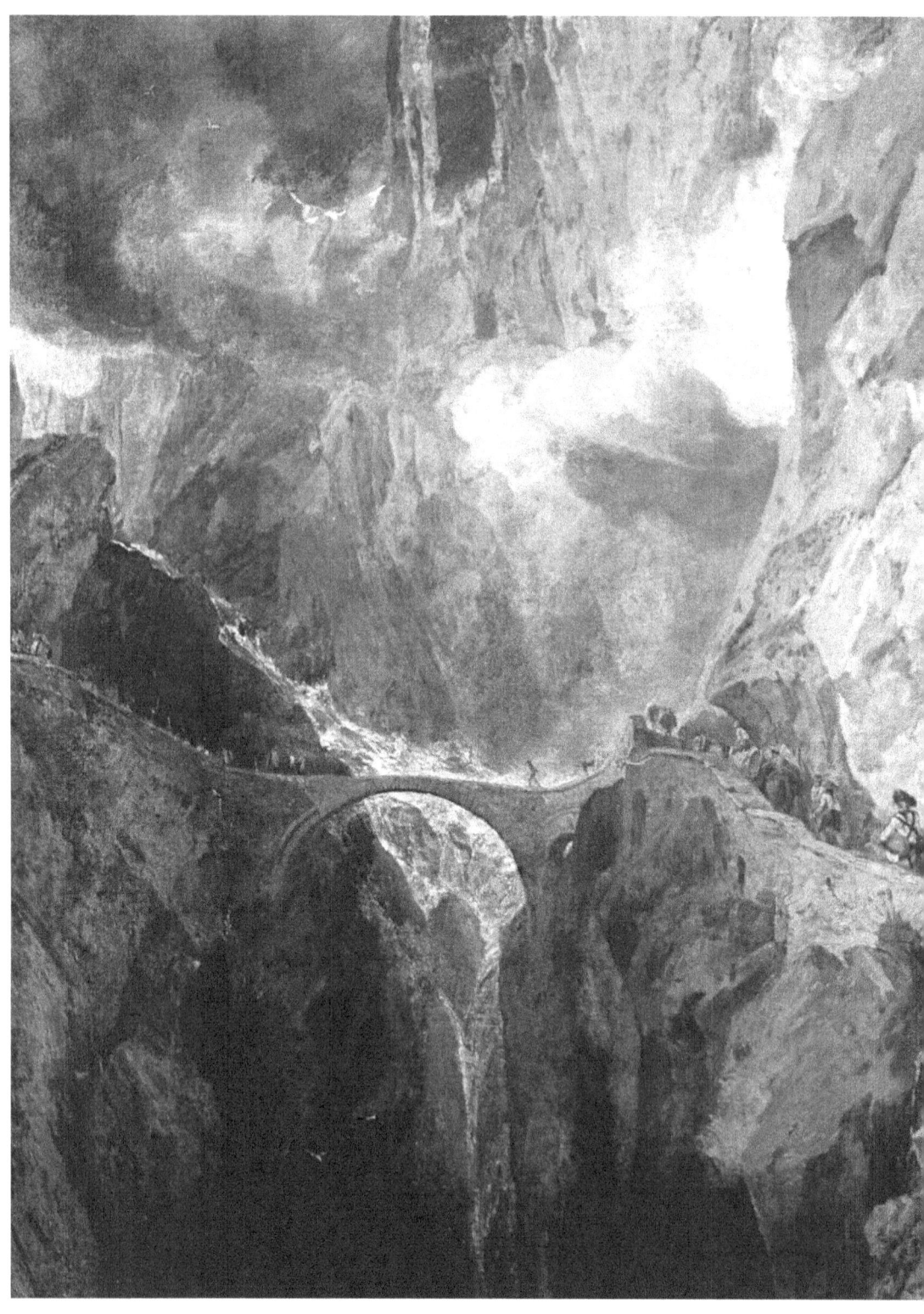

J.M.W. Turner, St Gothard Pass, 1804, Clore Gallery, London

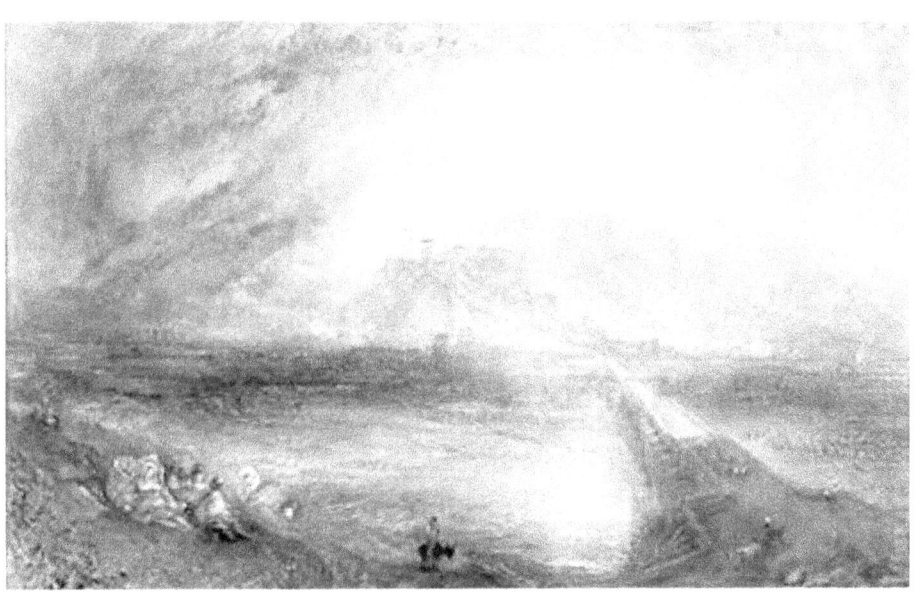

J.M.W. Turner, Bellinzona From the Road To Locarno, 1843

J.M.W. Turner, Lake of Lucerne, Clore Gallery, London

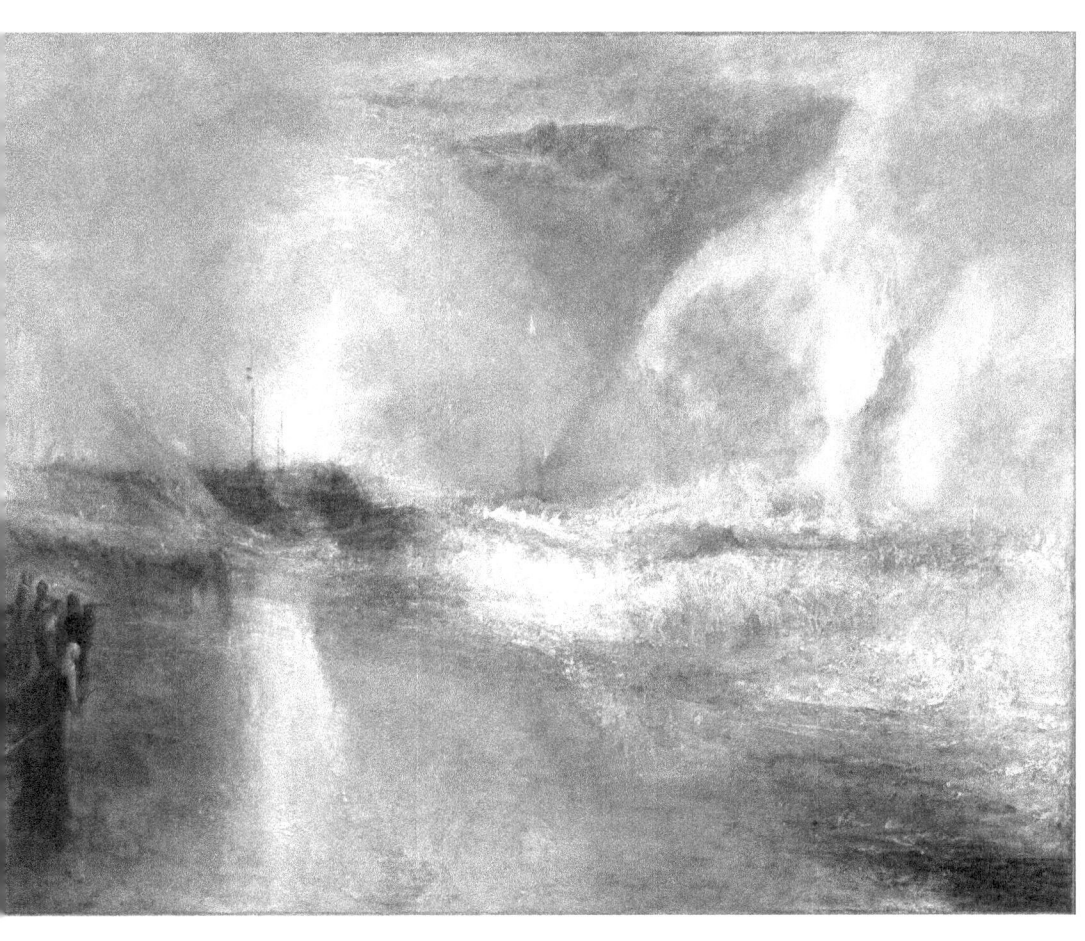

J.M.W. Turner, Rockets and Blue Lights (Close At Hand)
To Warn Steamboats of Shoal Water, Clark Art Institute

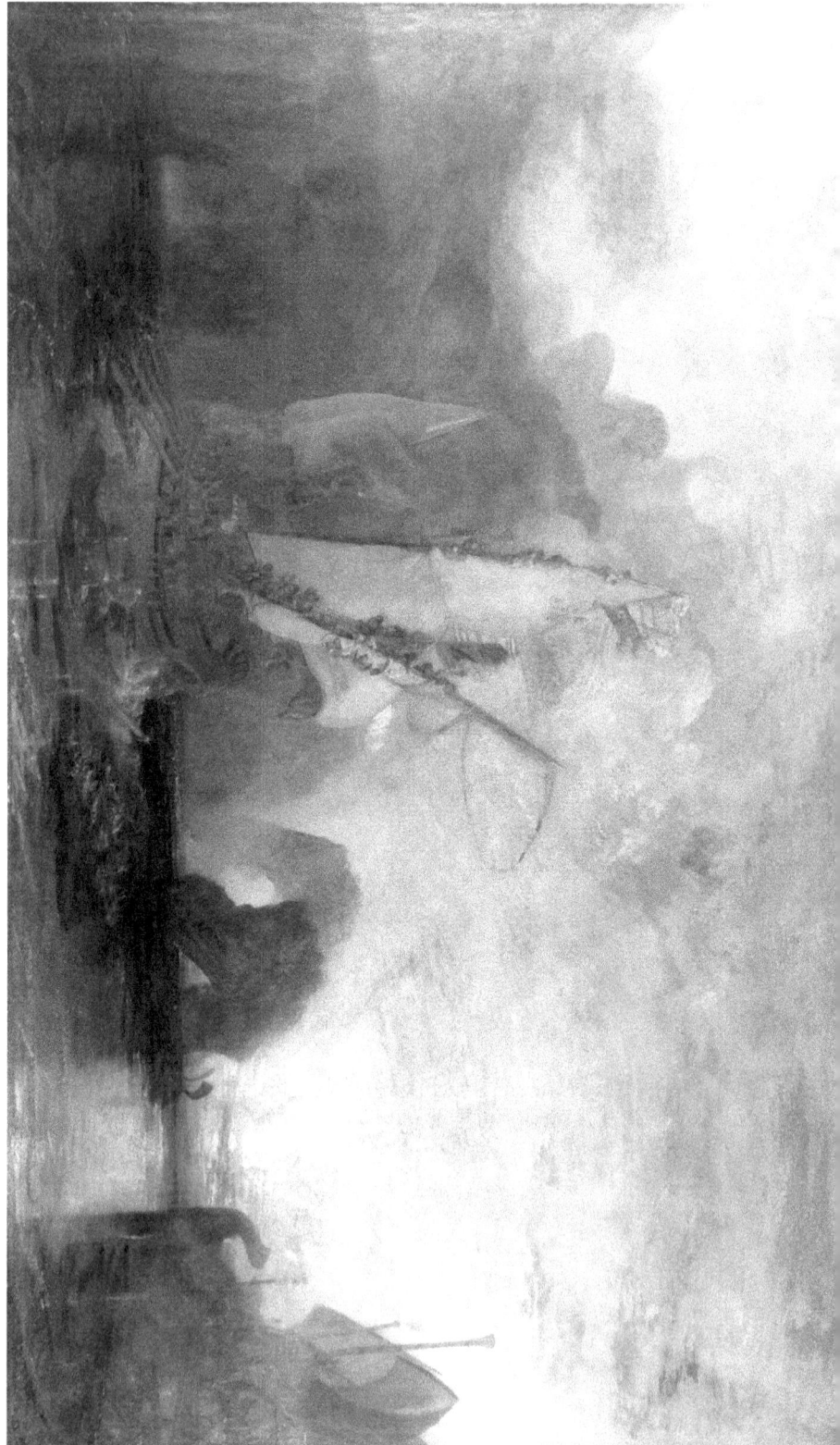

J.M.W. Turner, Ulysses Deriding Polyphemus, 1829, National Gallery, London

J.M.W. Turner, The Evening Star, 1830, National Gallery London

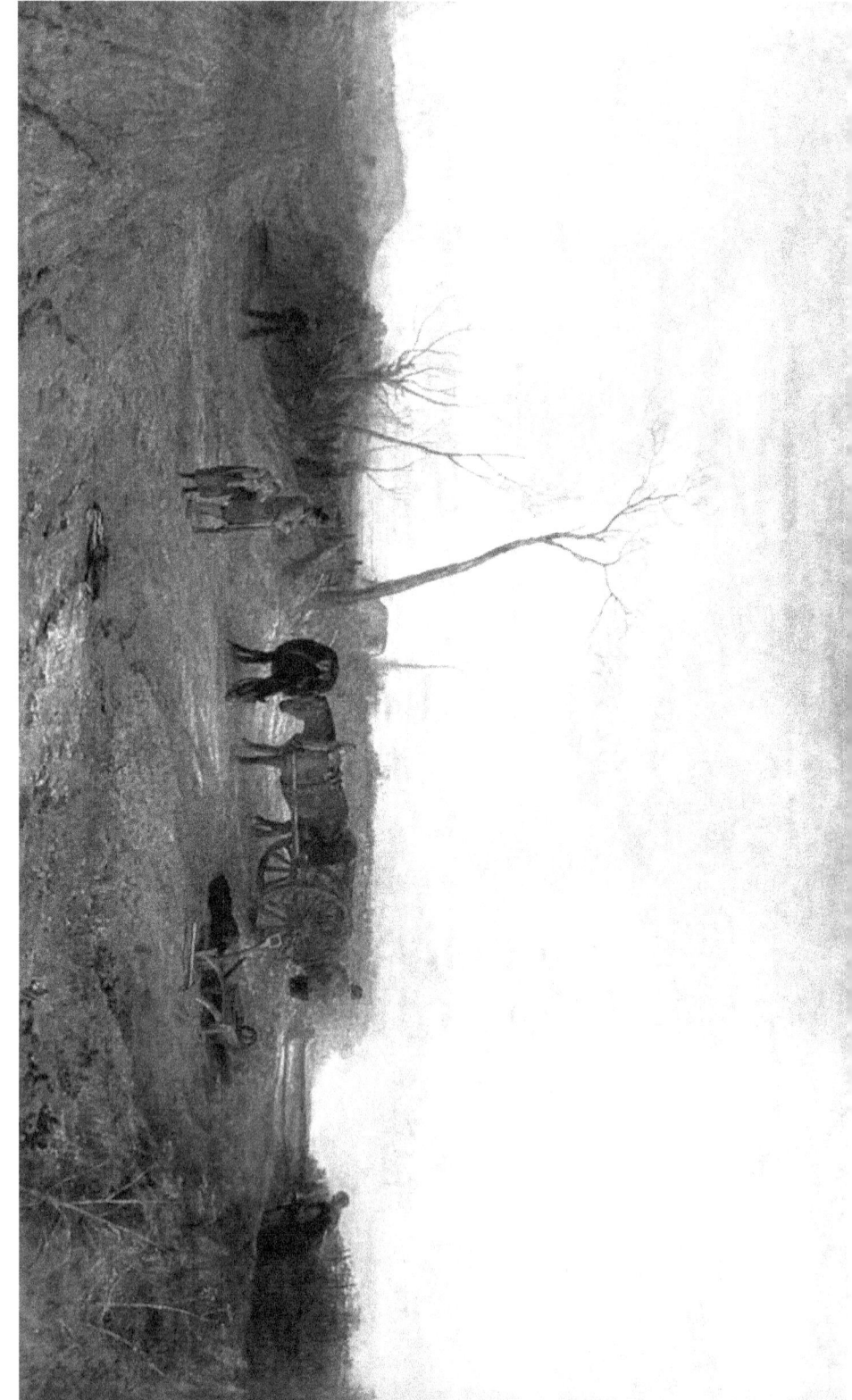

J.M.W. Turner, Frosty Morning, 1813, Clore Gallery

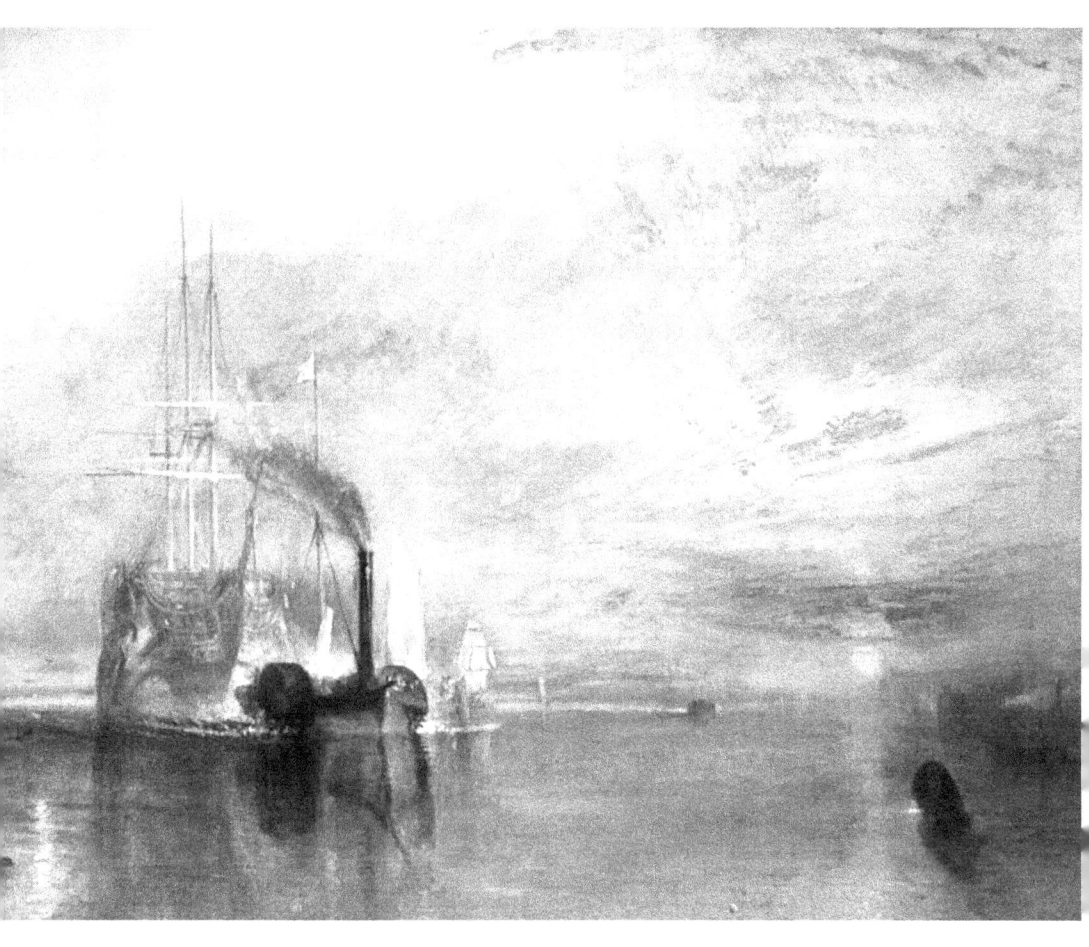

J.M.W. Turner, The Fighting Temeraire, 1839, London

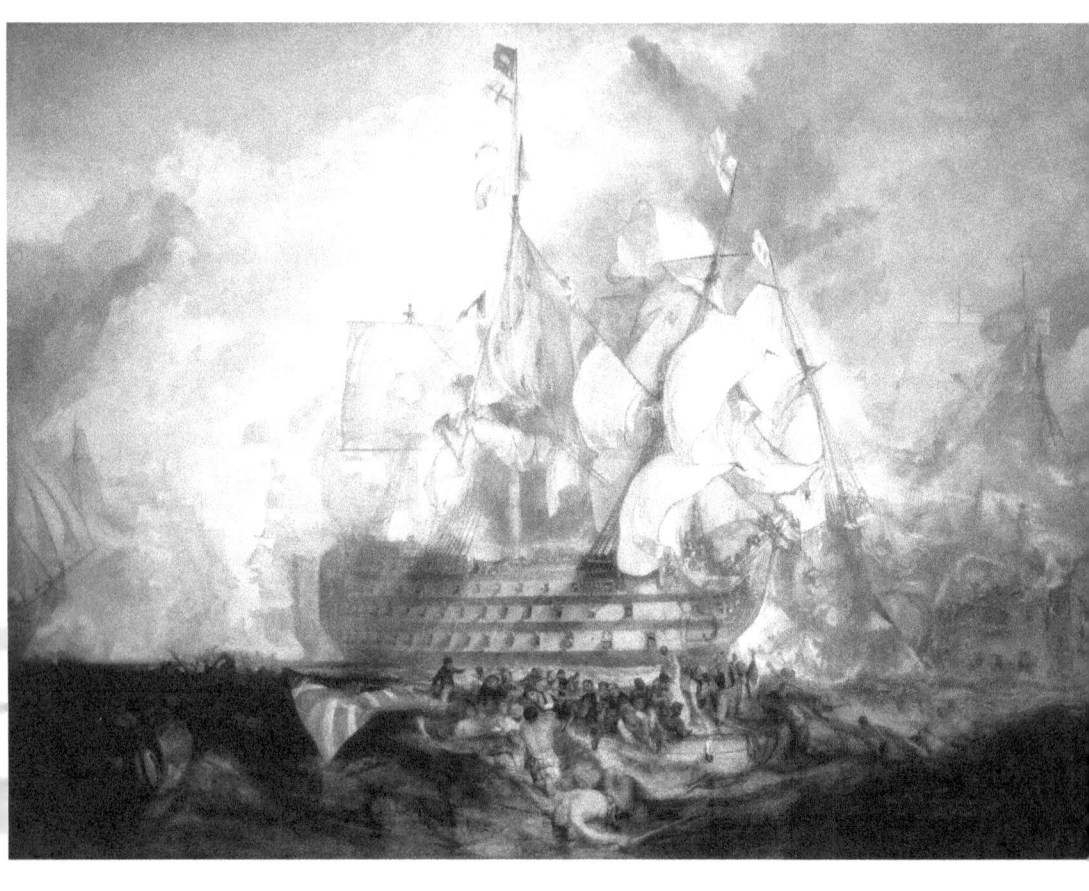

J.M.W. Turner, The Battle of Trafalgar, 1822, Greenwich

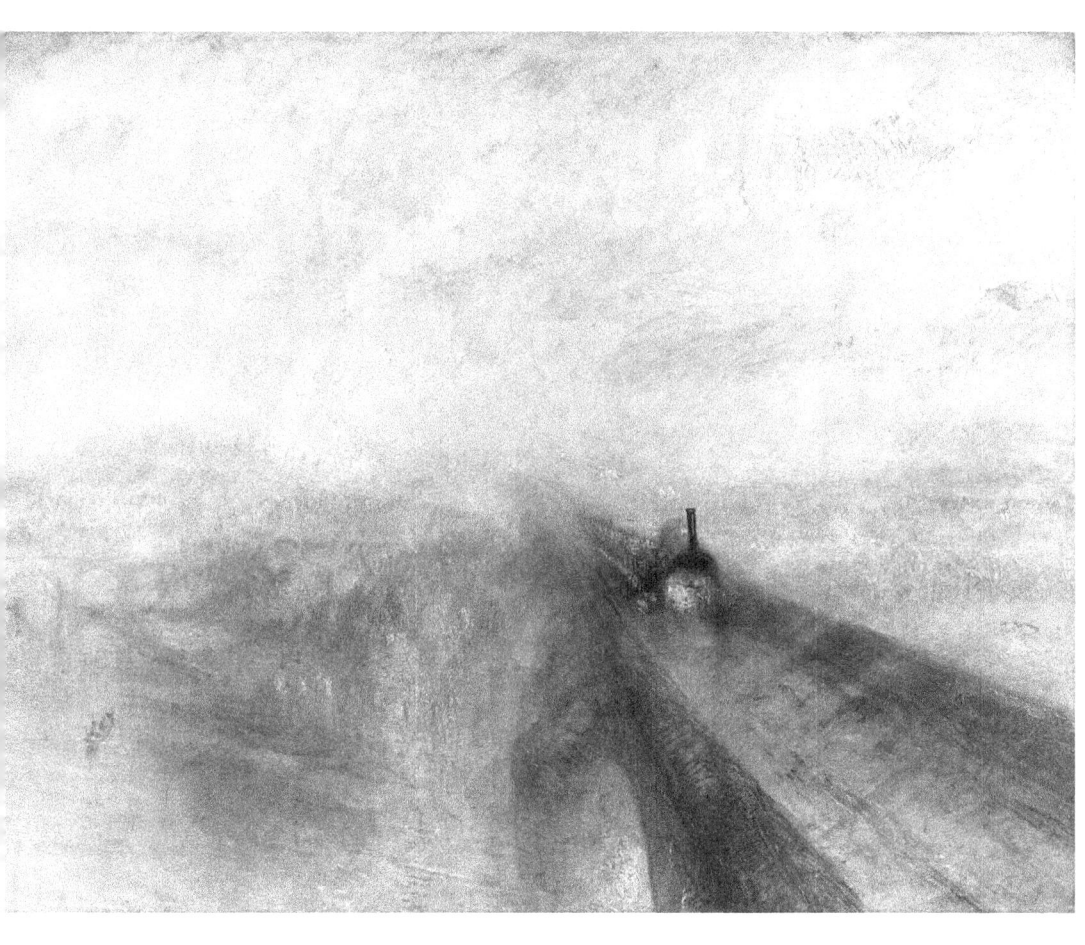

J.M.W. Turner, Rain, Steam and Speed, 1845, London

LETTER V

THE FLAME LEAPS, EXPANDS,
AND EXPIRES

When I think of Turner it is the later water-colours that flash
before me. The oils are magnificent, tremendous, wrought in
rivalry and for fame: the water-colours, lyrical impressions, moods
of elation inspired by beauty, are himself. We will go straight to
the six studies that hung on the wall by the fireplace, essential
effects selected with unerring instinct from the unessential, called
"Running Wave in a Cross-tide: Evening;" "Twilight on the Sea;"
"Sunshine on the Sea on a Stormy Evening;" "Breaking Wave on
Beach;" "Sunset on the Sea;" and "Coasting Vessels." The very
titles are lyrics. Yet they are not more beautiful than other
interpretations, pushed into the region where feeling and vision
merge into ecstasy – those I have already mentioned, and some,
my particular favourites, hanging on the wall to the left of
Ruskin's bust – the "Pilatus," the careful alchemy of "Carnarvon,"
and the atmospheric veils that part above the "Lake of Uri." Year
by year other of his water-colours shine out momentarily at
exhibitions, such as at the last Old Masters, when we saw the blue
and gold "Lake of Thun," and the visionary "Lake of Zug" about
which Ruskin wrote so enthusiastically in "Modern Painters"; and

the "apocalyptic splendour" of the "Zurich" at Messrs. Agnew's.

But one never reaches the end of his achievement in the National Gallery collection. A selection of the four hundred is permanently on view, but a greater number are stored in cabinets in an inner room, whence once in three months an assortment is withdrawn for exhibition. Apart from these there are the thousands of drawings and studies disinterred from the tin boxes which have been arranged chronologically by Mr. A. J. Finberg, in a hundred vast drawers, preparatory to his long labour on the *Catalogue Raisonné*.

Mark their range and you will realise that the whole world was his province. Think of the books he illustrated – the Rivers, Harbours, and Southern Coast Scenery of England, the Rivers of France, to name but four – travelling often on foot, with his luggage in a handkerchief tied to the end of a stick, flushing in the inn at night transparent washes of colour on paper, flowing tint into tint, knowing exactly what to do, sponging, scraping, using knife and finger, anything to force the material to express his vision. Once after a Rhine tour he appeared at Farnley Hall with a roll of fifty-three water-colours, painted at the rate of three a day.

I must show you the map of England and Scotland compiled by Mr. Huish, showing Turner's tours. It is covered with the lines of his tracks; you may see where he trudged or coached, and note the fourteen cathedrals, twenty-seven abbeys, and sixty-six castles which he drew. Similar maps might be made of France, Italy, and Switzerland.

Thinking of his wanderings, I look from the window of one of the Turner water-colour rooms near to the bust of Ruskin, who arranged and catalogued them; I look from the window and see a line of the new, dandy, taximeter cabs, and plan a little journey through London we two would take, if you were here. We would visit Van Tromp at the Soane, and then drive straight to the South Kensington Museum, where there are golden dreams by Turner such as the "Royal Yacht Squadron, Cowes"; but we would not tarry with the oils, for I should be impatient to show you the wall of water-colours, some behind protecting blinds, – the early "Wrexham," ageing houses and grey-blue tower; the perfect suggestion of the spirit of place called "Sketch of an Italian Town," and the fairy-like blue, gold, and purple "Lake of Brienz," pure flame of Turner.

Then we would speed to Millbank, enter the Tate Gallery, and stand in Room VII. where the recovered sunshine Turners hang in radiant array. Ruskin, you will remember, after Turner's death, separated the "finished from the unfinished." The "finished" are in the National Gallery; the "unfinished" are among the forty-four at Millbank. Fifty years ago they were deposited, hidden from public gaze, in the National Gallery; early in 1905 they were examined by order of the trustees, cleaned, restored, and found to be brilliant and fresh, as on the day when the greatest landscape painter the world has known, painted them.

These forty-four pictures should be sorted. Some show but the tumbling splendour of his decline when he fumbled with his visions, and produced such chaotic failures as the two Deluges, the "Burning Fiery Furnace," "The Angel standing in the Sun," "Undine," and "The Exile and the Rock Limpet." The holiday crowd, when I was last at the Tate Gallery, laughed as their forerunners laughed when the pictures were first exhibited. Their laughter enabled me to understand why Turner was secretive and boorish in old age, when his imagination outsoared his dwindling power to express his dreams in paint. Many visitors giggled and made flippant comments, just as *Punch* did when the old lion's eyes began to fail and his hand to tremble. Had Turner ceased painting when he was nearing seventy he might have been spared much, but he could not stop. His inward eye still saw gorgeous scenes, and amid the grime of his dingy house in Queen Anne Street he struggled with such unearthly themes as this Deluge in the evening and the morning, and Napoleon in the sunset of his exile. These are the pictures of his magnificent decline at which the crowd laughed, and at that riot of forms, so glorious in colour, called "Interior at Petworth." But they did not laugh at the "Norham Castle, Sunrise," a flush of the prismatic varieties of light against the blue mists of dawn, or at "The Evening Star," a nocturne thrown off long before Whistler popularised the word, done at the period when, the crepuscular hour of bats and owls obsessing Turner, he produced those small moonlight mezzotints, wonderful, dim, silver things, that were found in his house after he was dead. They did not laugh at the "Hastings," delicate blues and golden greys, with splendour in the upper sky, and the whole canvas aflame with the orange sail of the boat drawn up on the beach; or at the Yacht racing, an impression of sails against a tumbling sea, or at "A Ship Aground," the ground-swell rolling by the helpless vessel, and the sun setting angrily behind a bank of cloud; or at the Tivoli, an imaginative classical landscape probably painted as a pendant to the "Arch of Constantine." The setting suggests the scenery of Tivoli; but when Turner's imagination was fired, he cared little about topographical accuracy.

That day I waited until closing time, loth to leave these visions, noting with what art he had piled the chrome on the white ground in "Sunrise, with a Boat between Headlands," the delicacy of the faint hues, the gold in the sky, the gold on the cliff, splashed yonder with blue, and the golden boat sailing ever on.

The hour drew near five. The attendant appeared, drew the curtains one by one over the sunshine pictures, hiding them with red hangings, all but the four large valedictory scenes from classical mythology, and the other splendid failures which have no curtains.

When I left the Gallery and stood upon the terrace overlooking the Thames and thence towards Chelsea, I saw, in the mind's eye, the print published after Turner's death that I had picked years ago from a twopenny portfolio in the Brompton Road, showing the little house by Cremorne Pier where he died, under the assumed name of Booth. The sun shines upon the building. The Thames flows in front of it. It is said that as long as strength held he would rise at daybreak, and wrapped in a blanket, stand upon the roof watching the colour flush the eastern sky.

The Chelsea hiding-place was discovered, but he was sinking when a friend found him. He died on December 18, 1851, at the window, looking upon the river, propped upon his couch. A full, and, I think, with occasional lapses – the lot of all – a happy life, for his work never ceased to be less than absorbing. He died in the light, having run his race to the goal.

The account of that dinner at David Roberts' house, not long before his death, when he tried to propose his host's health, "ran short of words and breath, and dropped down in his chair, with a hearty laugh, starting again, and finishing with a 'hip, hip, hurrah!'" shows that the power to enjoy, and the sense of fun, had not withdrawn from the solitary genius, the "very moral of a master carpenter, with lobster red face, large fluffy hat and enormous umbrella," who wrestled with the sun, read Ovid, and Young's "Night Thoughts," tramped Europe in pursuit of beauty, and who was seen on the old Margate steamer studying the movement of the water, and the boiling foam in the wake of the "Magnet," and making his luncheon off shrimps strewn over an immense red handkerchief spread across his knee – Turner.

POSTSCRIPT

TURNER AND TWO OTHERS

Climbing the stairs to the flat, I passed a girl who was toiling upwards.

Pressing the button of the electric bell I watched her ascend the last flight. She paused. I inferred that our destination was the same, noted that she carried a satchel, a thick notebook, and a paper-covered sixpenny reprint. Mildly curious as to the title of the novel, I dissembled, and read "Endeavours after the Christian Life," by James Martineau. Therewith the stone staircase faded away, the stone walls opened to the past, and I saw my youth, and the figure of my father returning one night to the old home, his face illumined, his eyes shining; heard again the earnest words between him and my mother; how he had been at Martineau's valedictory address, how with the teacher's commun- ication telling of deep things of the spirit moving within him he had avoided friends, unable to return suddenly to earth, and how he had walked home as if with wings. Those were the days when the "Endeavours" was a costly, exclusive, and some-what revolutionary book. A few quick years, and lo! it becomes one of Allenson's sixpenny series, bought by the hundred thousand.

The door of the flat opened, Martineau slept again with his

forefathers, the saints of all time, and the girl and I passed into the modest room dedicated to one who was no saint. Yet I do not know. If a saint be he who by his life makes this world for others more wonderful, more beautiful and better worth living in, then Joseph Mallord William Turner was a saint. Which is strange.

I did not speak of saints to our hostess, for Turner is her god, and a god is greater than a half-god. There is one severe note in her room – the bust of Cæsar on a pedestal; all the rest is beauty – sheer beauty. I wonder what a far-horizon Colonial, who had never seen Turner's later water-colours, would feel in this room; walls covered with sensitive copies of those flushes of radiant colour, waning blue dawns, purple mysteries of eve, sunlighted Swiss lakes, dream buildings, rainbow reaches of the Rhine, opalescent distances stretching past headlands into infinity.

The head of Cæsar, from his tall pedestal, surveyed these lyrics in colour, as strange to him as would have been the "Endeavours after the Christian Life," that paper book, tightly clutched, hidden from view, in a girl's hand. Then twilight came, the lamp was lighted, and I went away to carry out an idea that had just shaped itself.

I had never seen the house in Queen Anne Street where Turner lived with Mrs. Danby and the cats. Should I find the house changed – houses rather, for he owned three, two in Harley Street, and one in Queen Anne Street, communicating mysteriously at the back, and leaving the corner building in other hands.

As I walked through the Bloomsbury Squares I thought not of Turner, but of another, a man, very old, very frail, bent almost double, with the face of a spirit and the eye of a seer, whom years ago I had met on this very spot, creeping round the railings which encircle the grass and trees – James Martineau, still lingering in the world which his spirit had long outsoared. I saw, in the mind's eye, that shrivelled octogenarian figure, and I asked at three shops for the "Endeavours after the Christian Life," found it in the fourth, and under lamp-post and by lighted windows, turned the familiar pages and read fragments.

The chapter headings stirred old thoughts, and there was one passage in the discourse on "Immortality" that seemed the voice of the dead murmuring as I went westward through the dark squares, saying that we see here only the partial operation of a higher law, that we witness no extinction, but simply migrations of the mind, which survives to fulfil its high offices elsewhere, and find perhaps in seeming death its true nativity.

As I walked that voice stilled the tumult of the traffic, companioned me through unfamiliar streets, until I knew by the brass plates on the doors, and the lighted rooms shining through holland blinds in upper stories, that I was in Harley Street, and near to Turner's house. Which was it?

A frock-coated, shining-hatted, prosperous personage, carrying a small black bag, was inserting a latch-key in one of the brass plate doors. As I advanced, his black bag swung up to cover his watch-chain.

"Which was Turner's house?" said I.

"Turner! What Turner? Was he a medical man?"

"No! the great Turner, I mean the Painter."

He collected himself, reflected, and said: "Ah! I do remember something! Yes, there is a tablet on the house yonder."

I peered up at the dwelling and saw, half way to the roof, a medallion, and the lamplight shining upon the first letters of the name Turner. This was the house of him who interpreted the feel of Nature, the movement of sea and wind, the glory of the sun, the mystery of its veiled face, the pomp of the world, the magic influence of light so transcendently that we say: "Yes! this magician was initiate! This queer Englishman was near to the eternal dream of his Maker."

As I stood in the dark street and looked up at Turner's house, the Shades gathered about me. A wizard in words joined this son of a London barber, and that saint whose works have gone into a sixpenny edition.

This was the house that Ruskin knew. Behind these walls,

were stored the pictures and water-colours in praise of which the most eloquent, the most inspiring, the most wilful and bewildering book that has ever been written upon art, was composed. Book? A library! The index alone of "Modern Painters" fills one volume. On the doorstep of this house Turner once stood and said to his disciple, who was about to start forth on a foreign tour – "Don't make your parents anxious. They'll be in such a fidge about you." He did not understand literary enthusiasm, and I doubt if he ever read a page of the copy of "The Stones of Venice" that Ruskin presented to him.

Three ghosts in a walk through London! Three great figures that trailed through the nineteenth century – a wizard in paint, a wizard in words, a wizard in holiness. Which is the greatest? Ruskin and Martineau explained, taught, chided, interpreted, and uplifted. Turner just acted, was content merely to express himself, to state his wonder at the wonder of the world. Is not his influence the most enduring? A man of few words and those mostly incoherent, who taught nothing, believed nothing, gazed on the sun with hope, and did superhuman things. His prayers were his pictures.

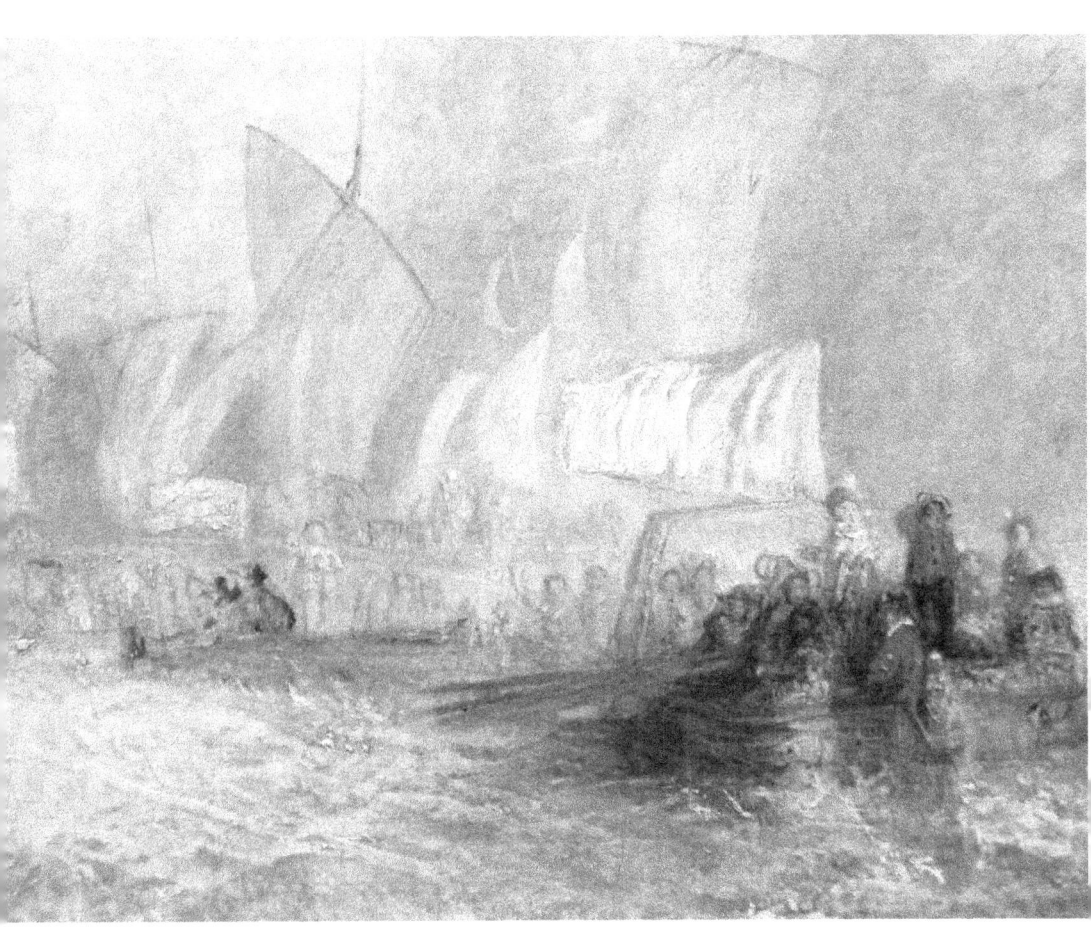

J.M.W. Turner at the Getty in L.A.
(This page and over).

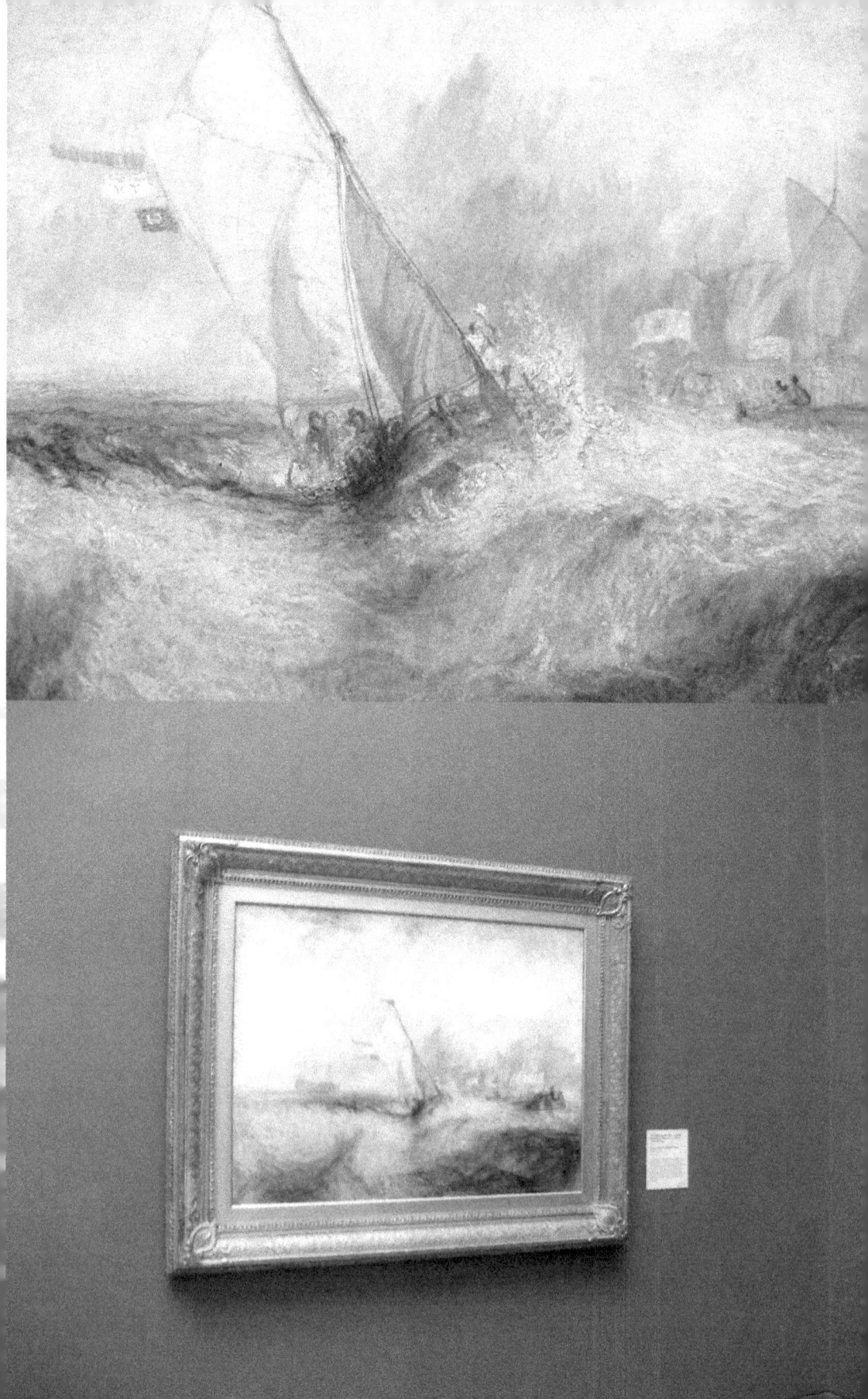

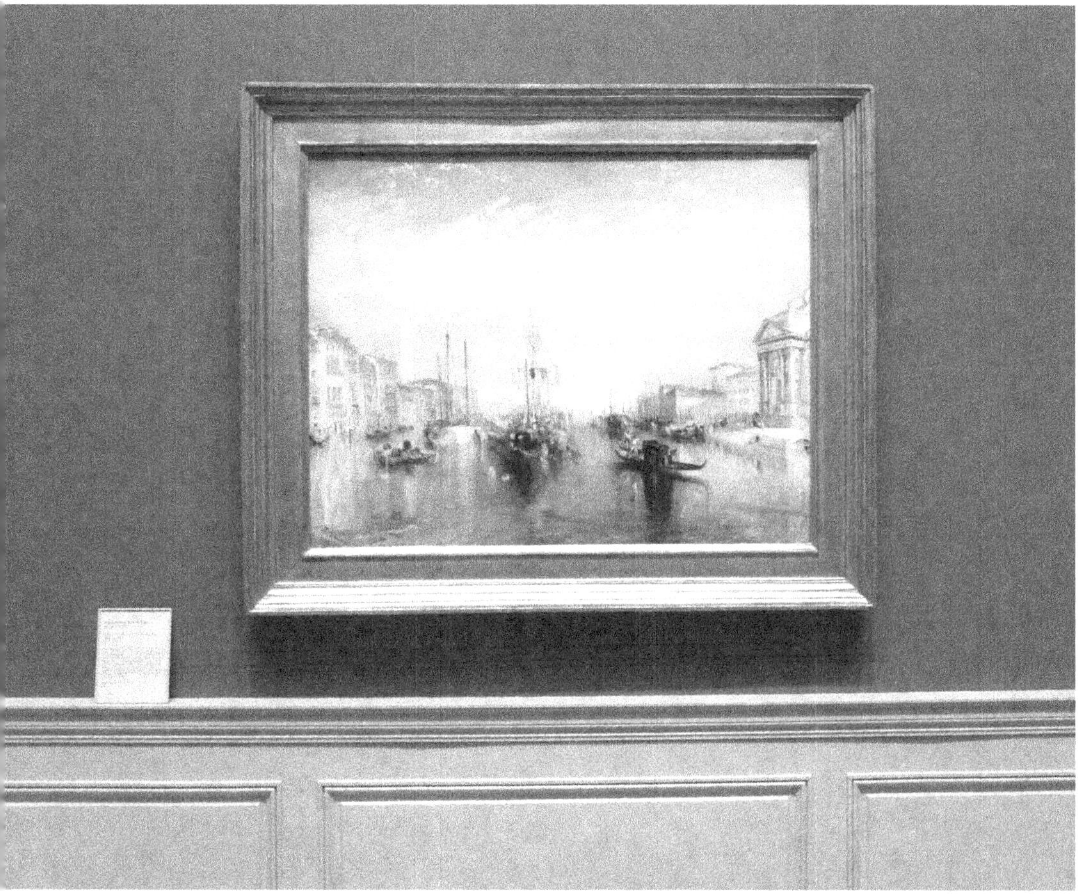

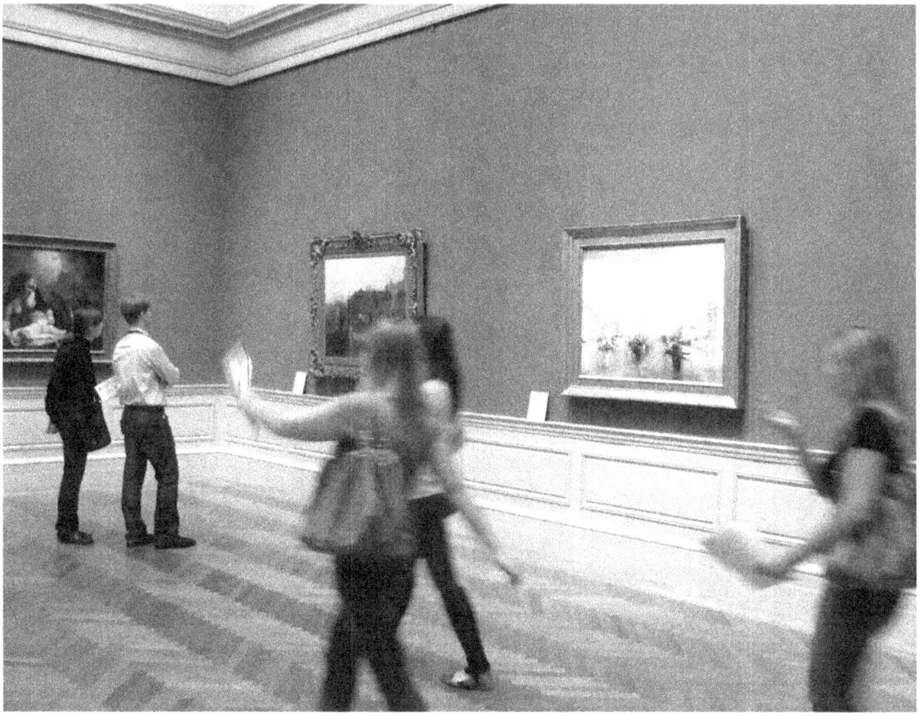

J.M.W. Turner in Gotham, at the Met (this page and over).
Venice From the Porch of the Madonna della Salute, 1830-35.

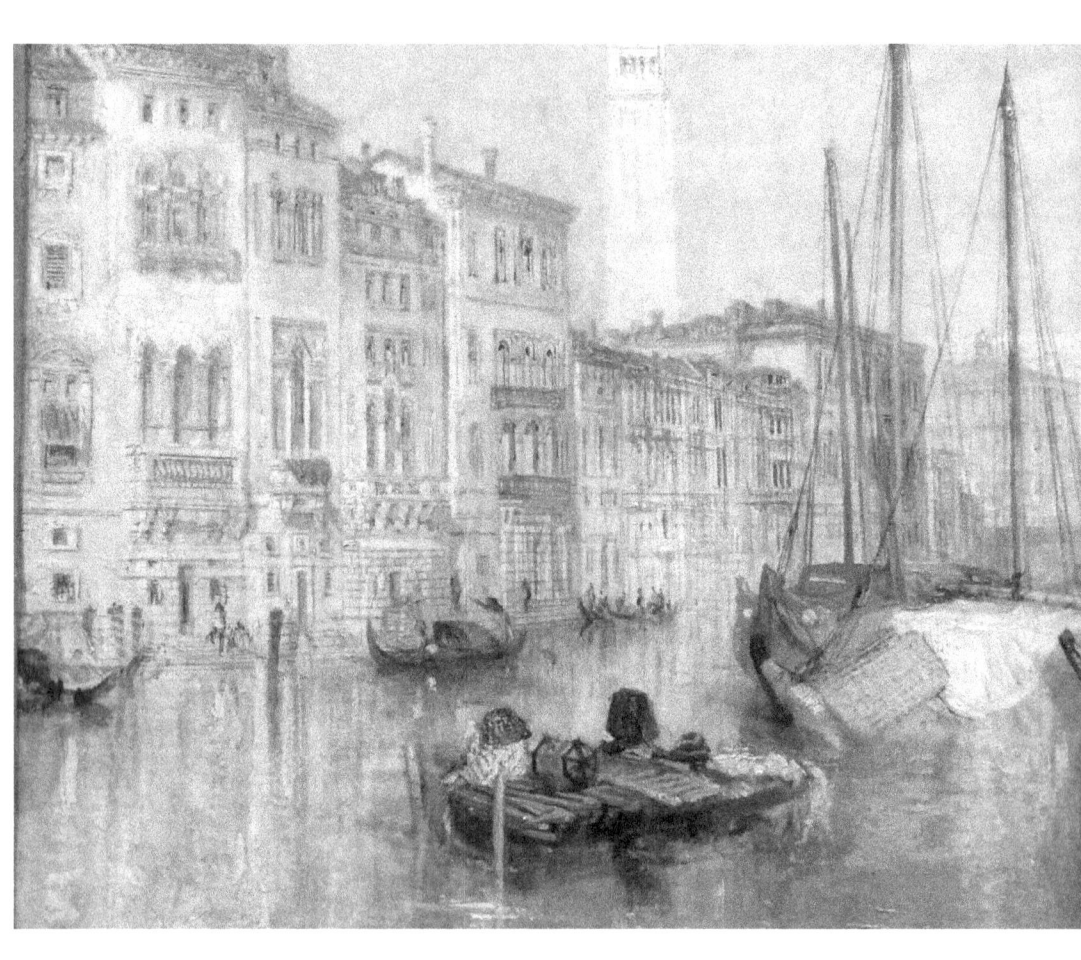

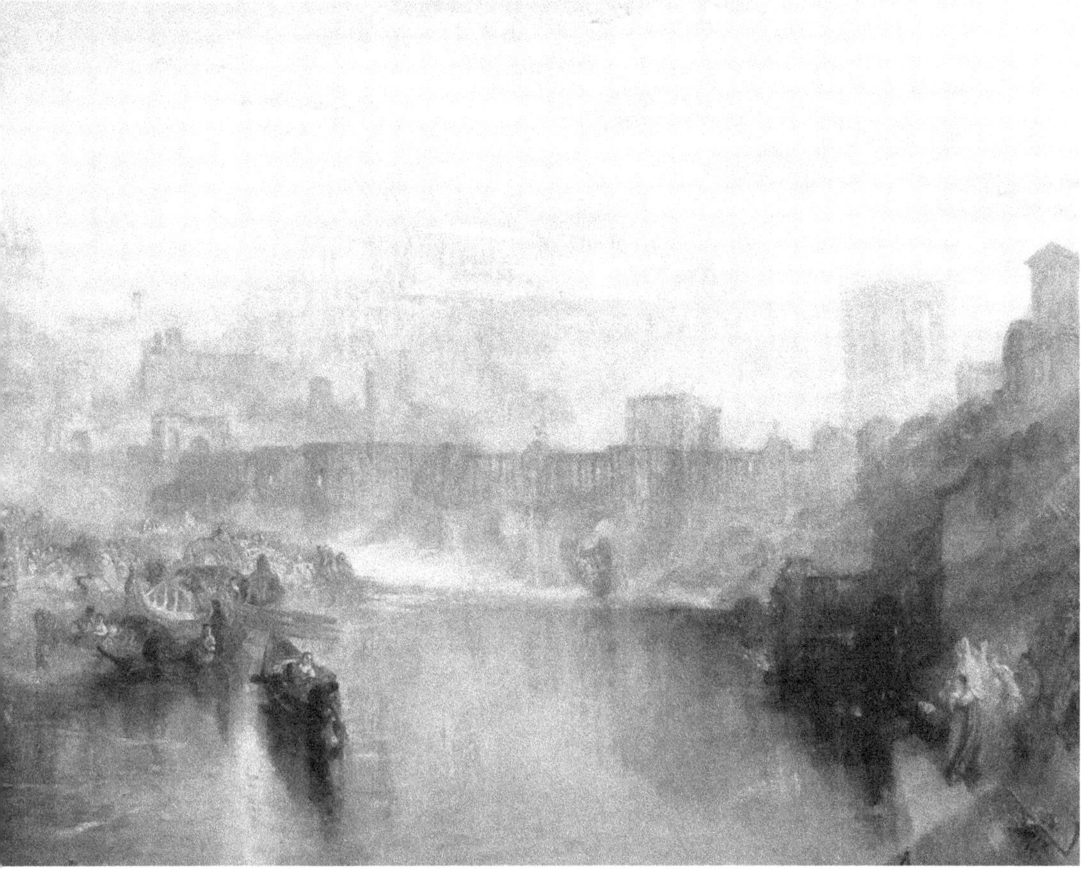

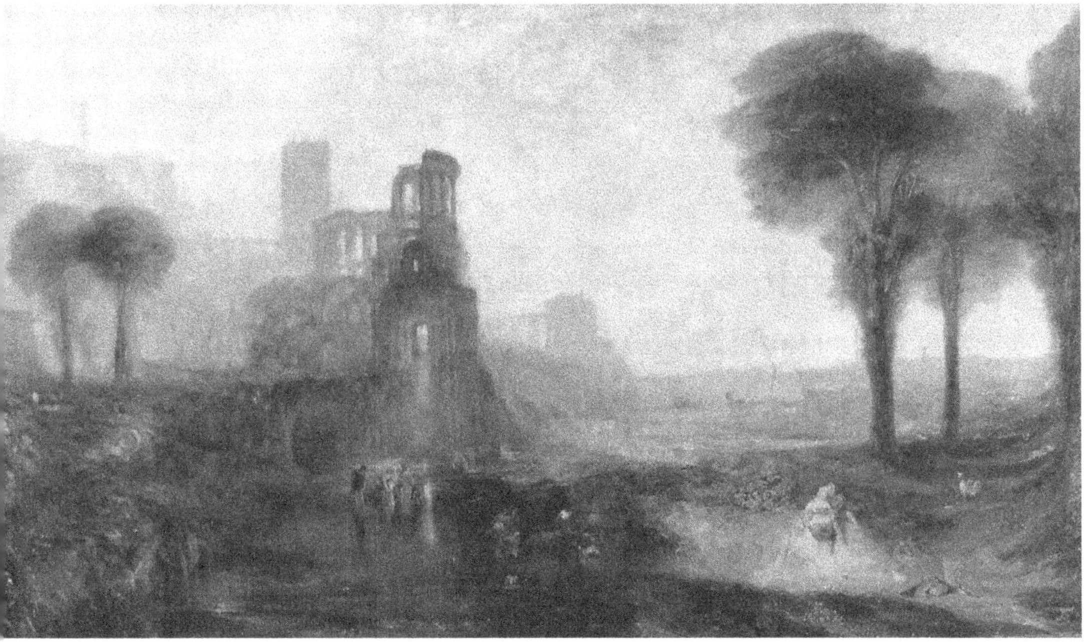

J.M.W. Turner, Ancient Rome, 1839 (top).
Caligula's Palace, 1831 (above). Both Clore Gallery.

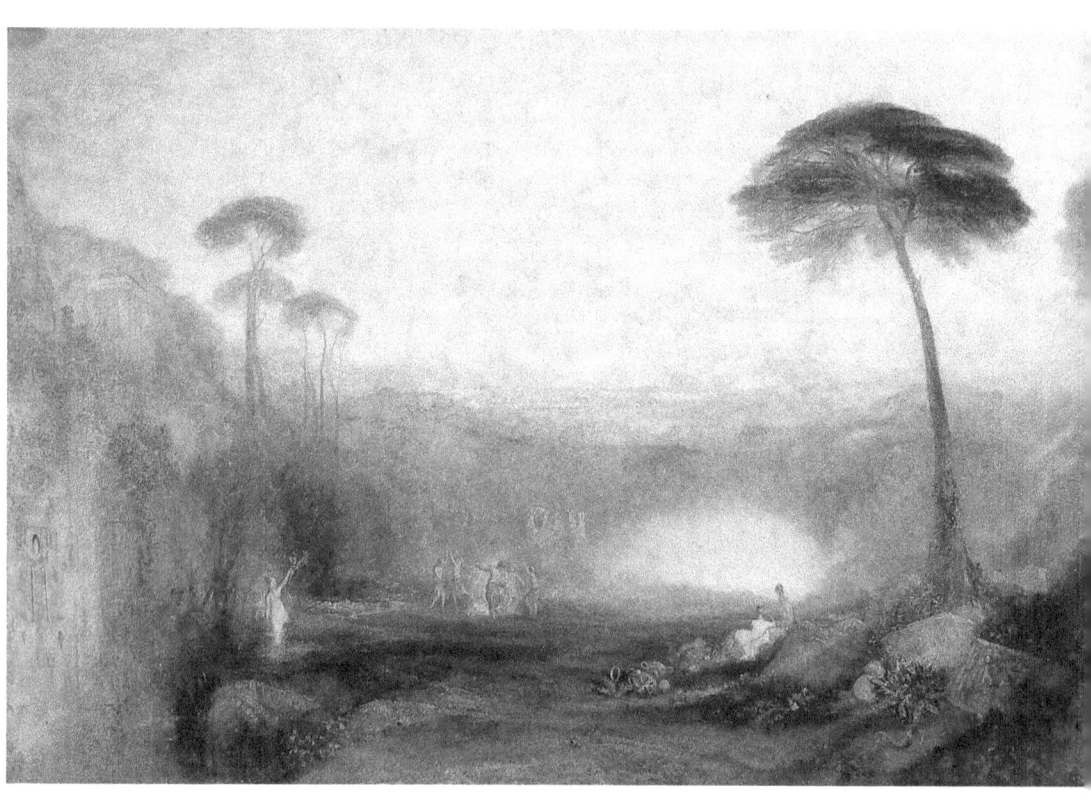

J.M.W. Turner, The Golden Bough, 1834, Clore Gallery

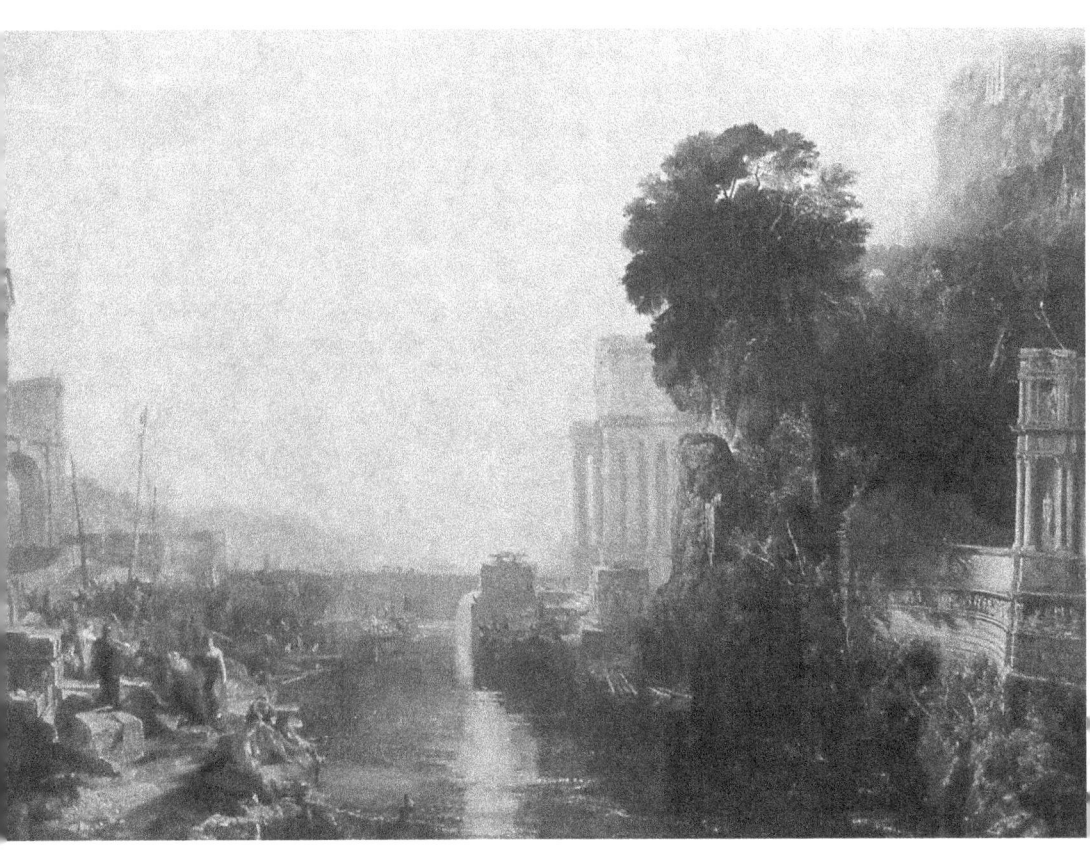

J.M.W. Turner, Dido Building Carthage, 1815, National Gallery, London

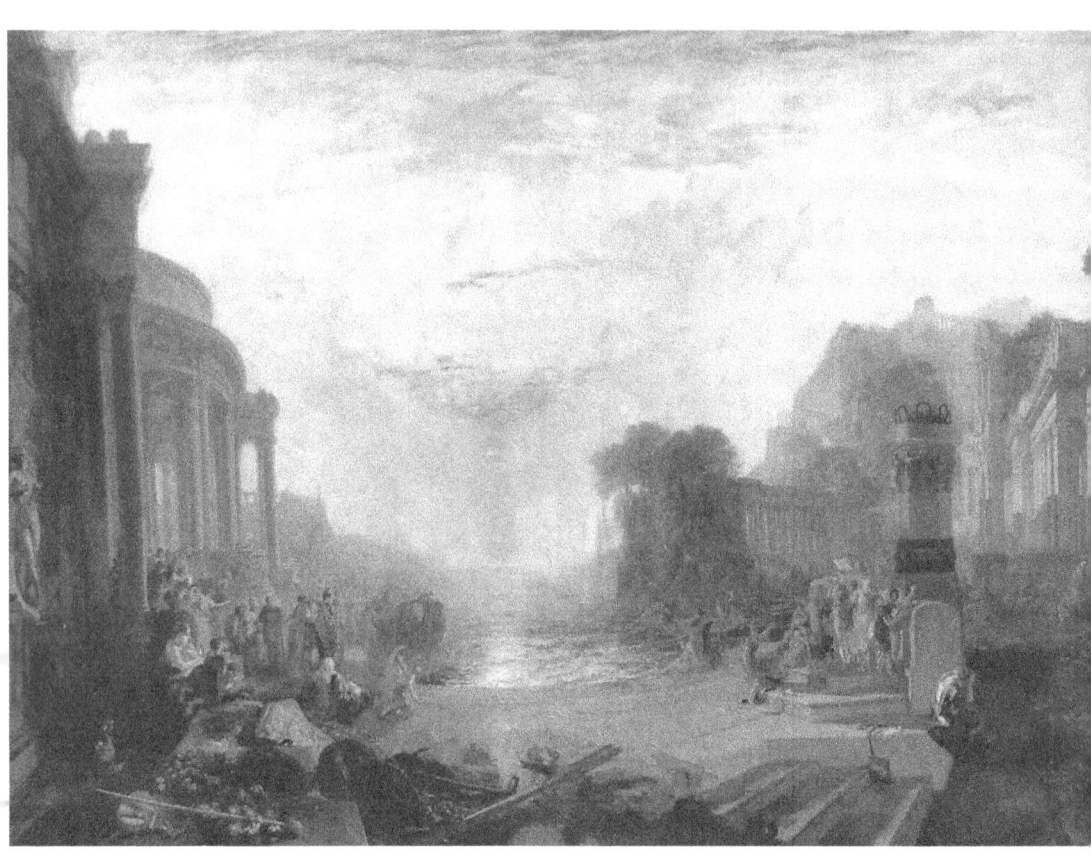

J.M.W. Turner, The Decline of the Carthaginian Empire, 1817, Clore Gallery

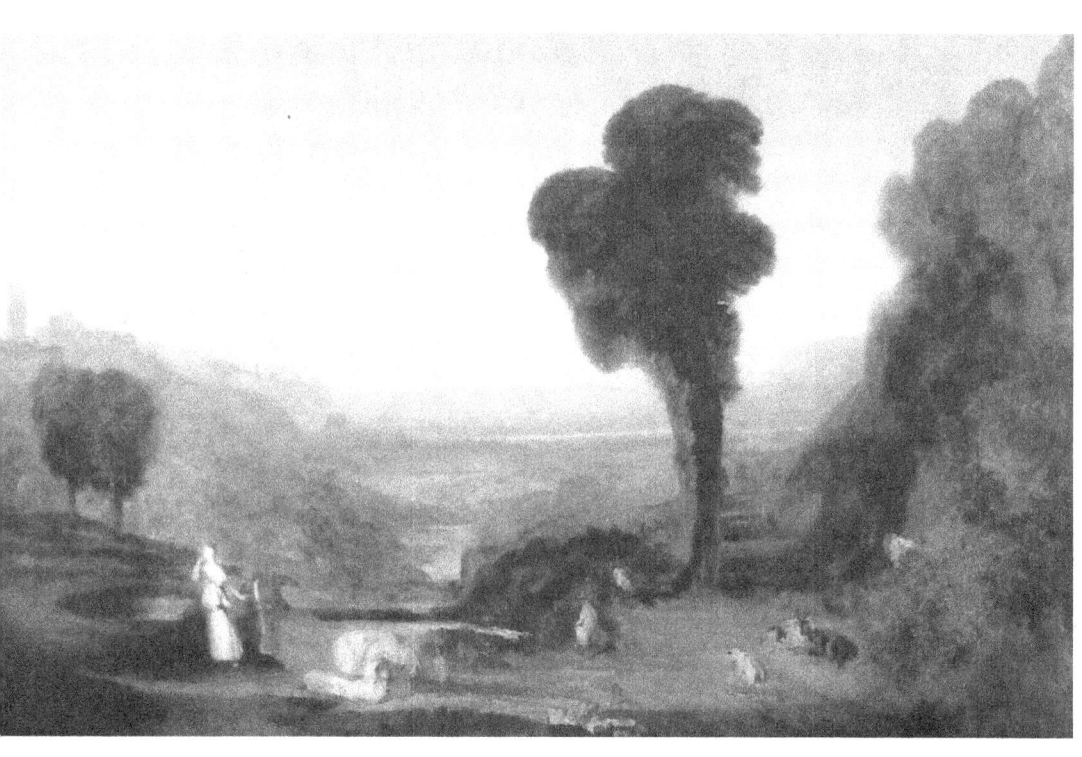

J.M.W. Turner, Landscape With Christ, c. 1825, Clore Gallery

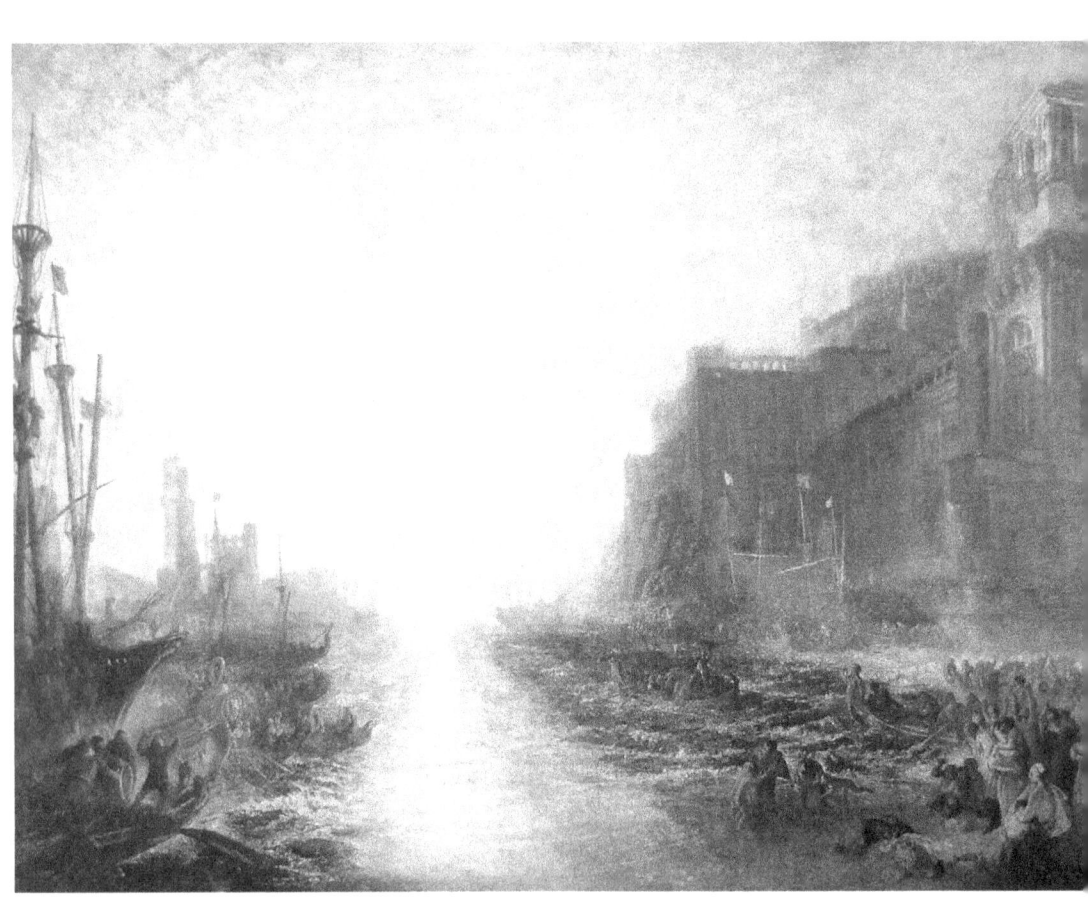

J.M.W. Turner, Regulus, 1828/ 1837, Clore Gallery

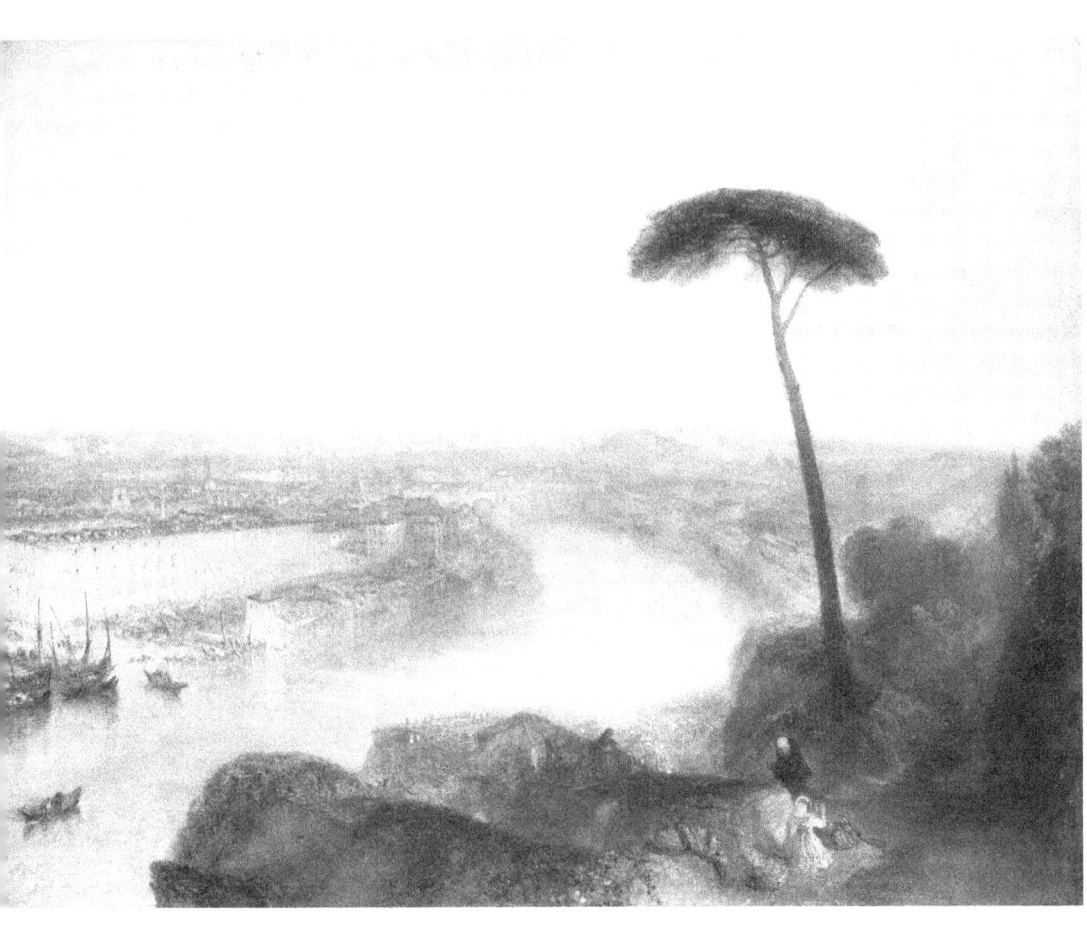

J.M.W. Turner, Rome, From Mount Aventine, late 1820s, private collection

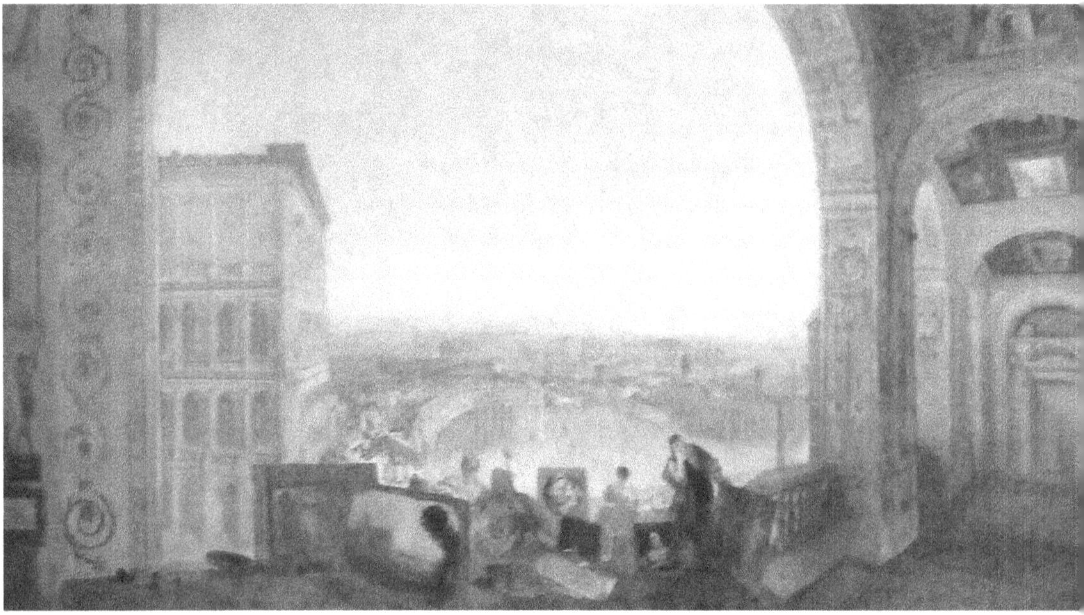

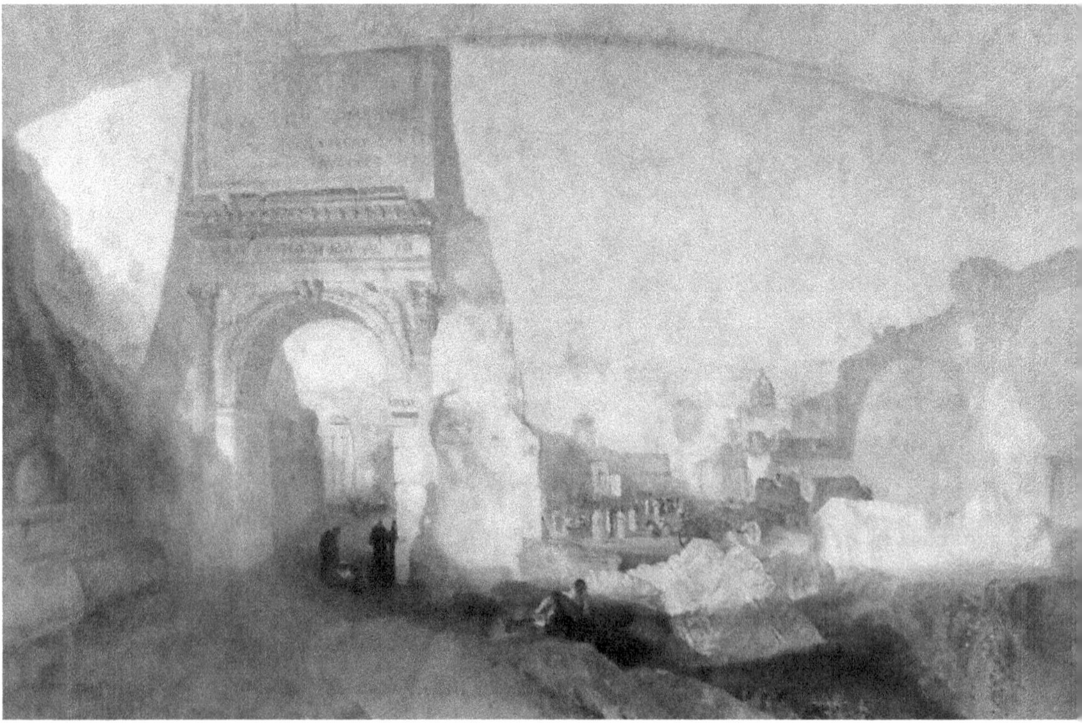

J.M.W. Turner, Rome From the Vatican, 1820 (top).
Forum Romanum, 1826 (above). Both Clore Gallery.

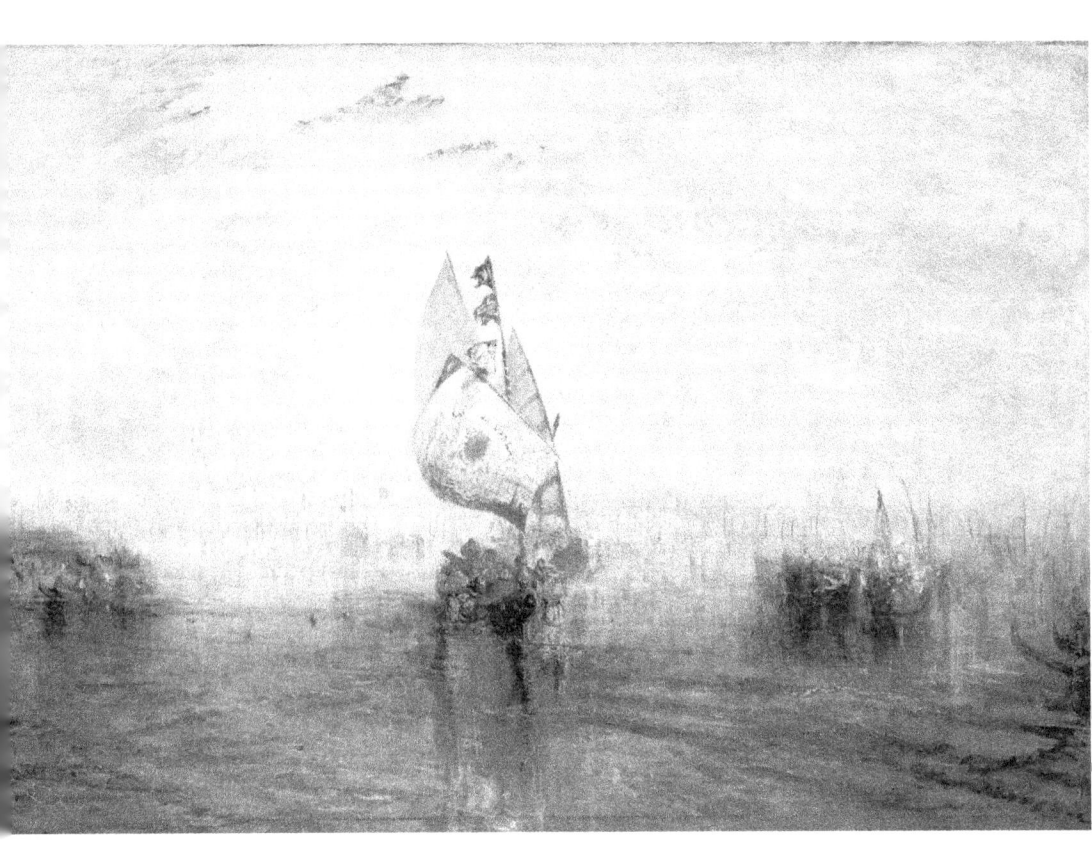

J.M.W. Turner, The Sun of Venice Going To Sea, 1843, Clore Gallery

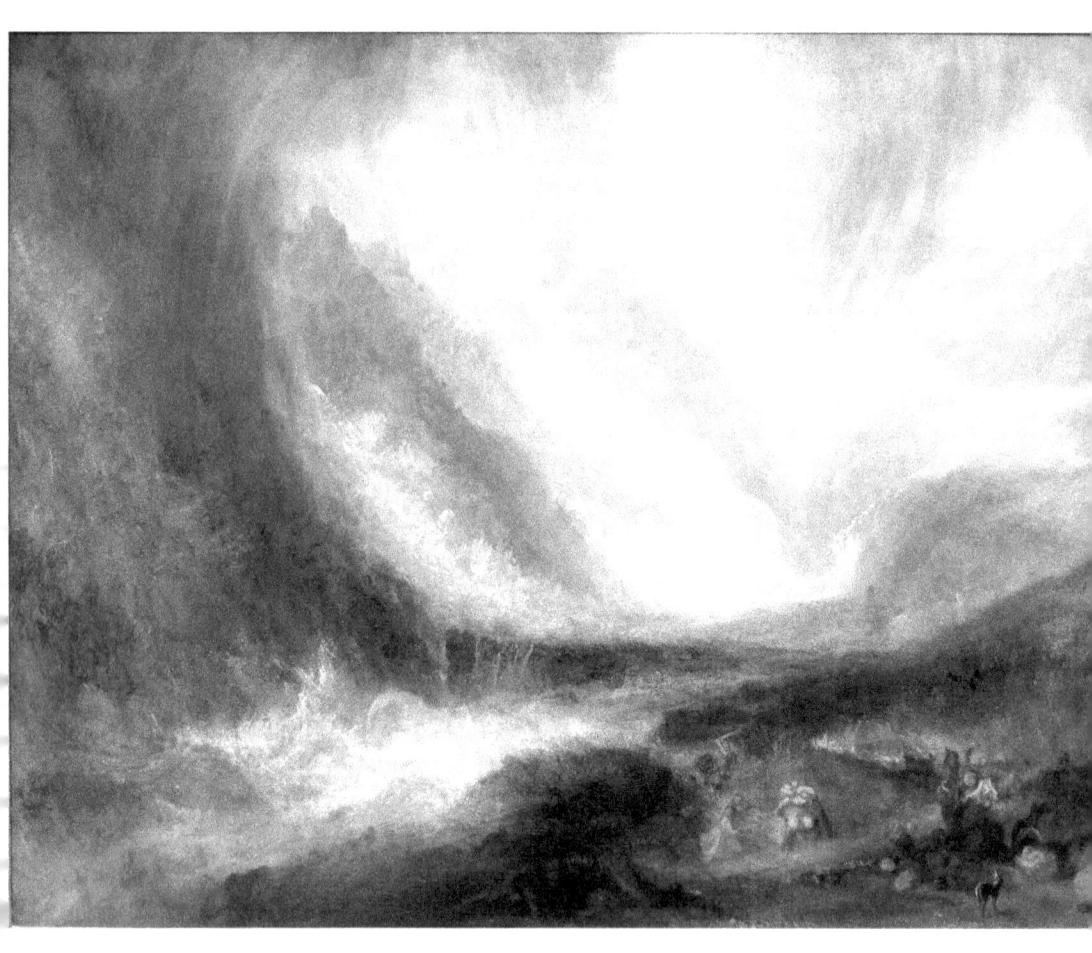

J.M.W. Turner, Valley Aosta, 1836-37, Chicago

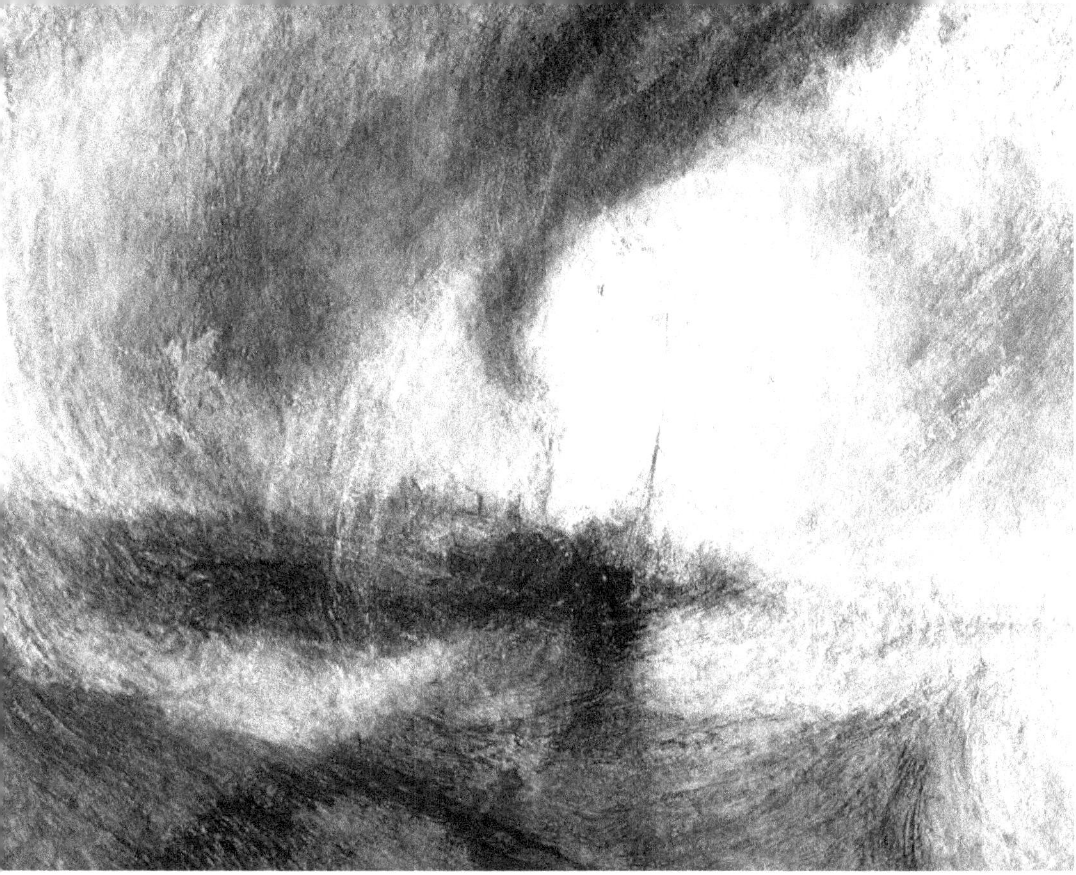

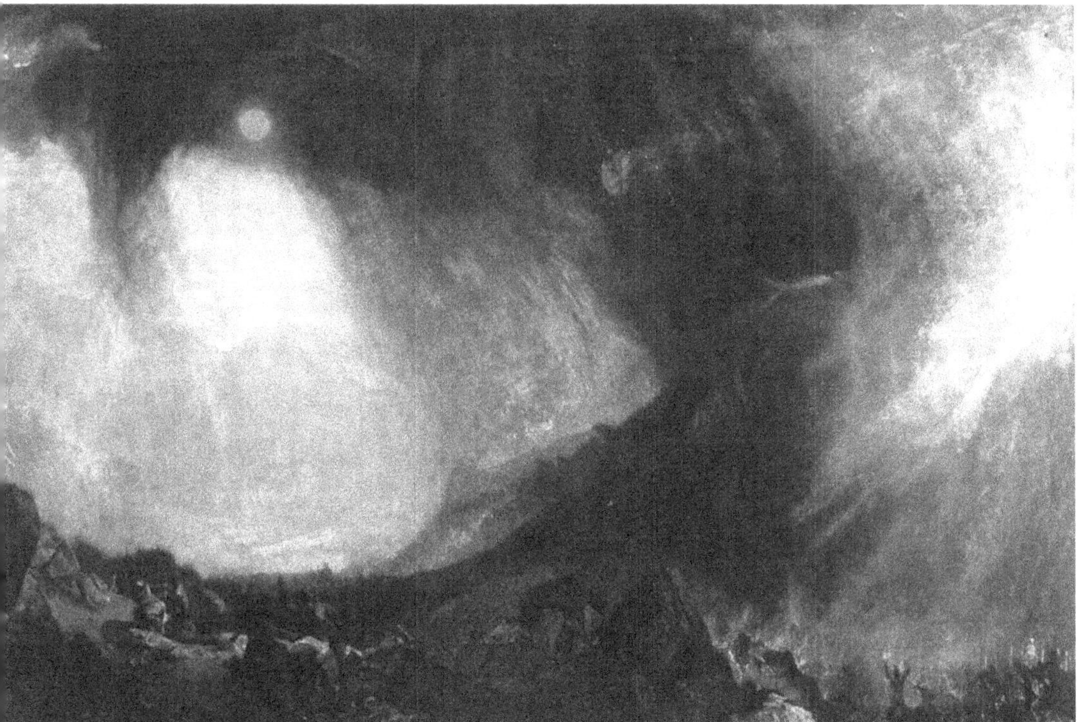

J.M.W. Turner, Snowstorm, 1842 (top).
Snowstorm, Hannibal and His Army Crossing the Alps, 1812 (above). Both Clore Gallery.

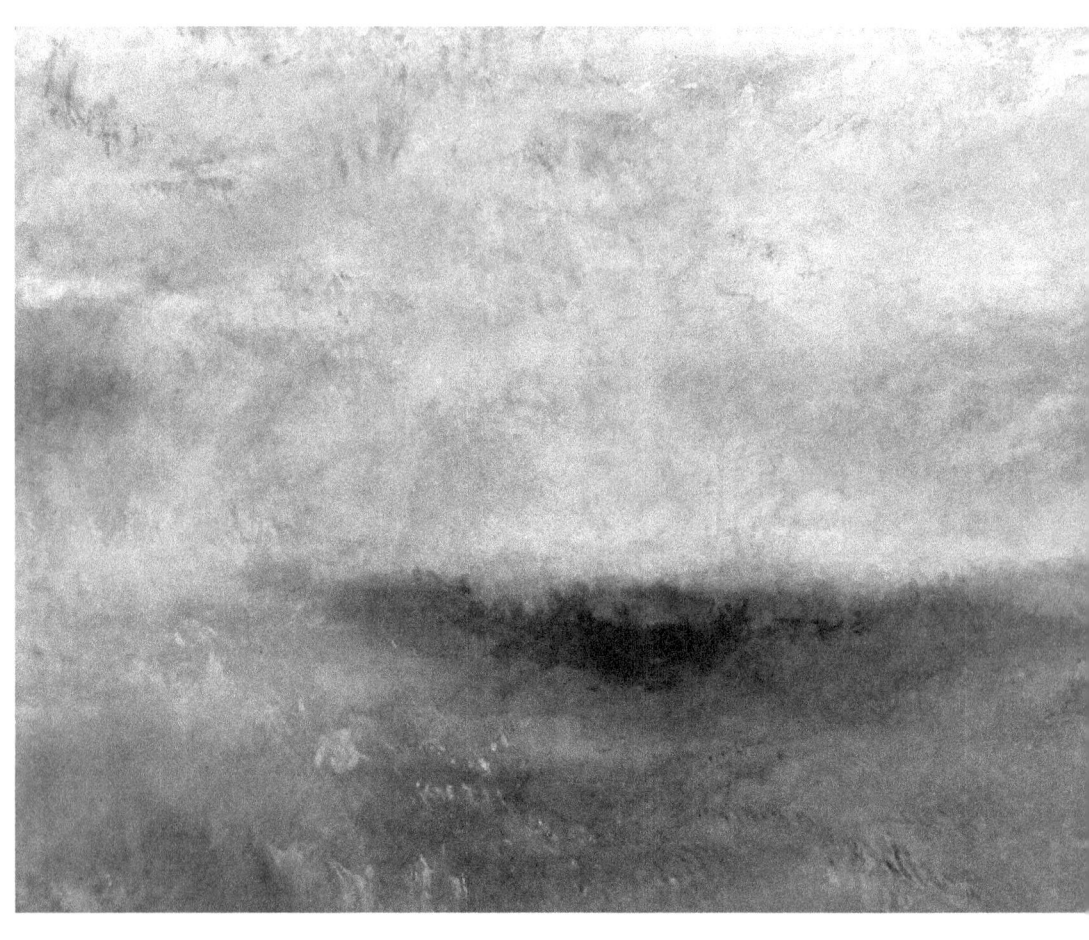

J.M.W. Turner, Sea With Storm Coming On, c. 1840, Clore Gallery

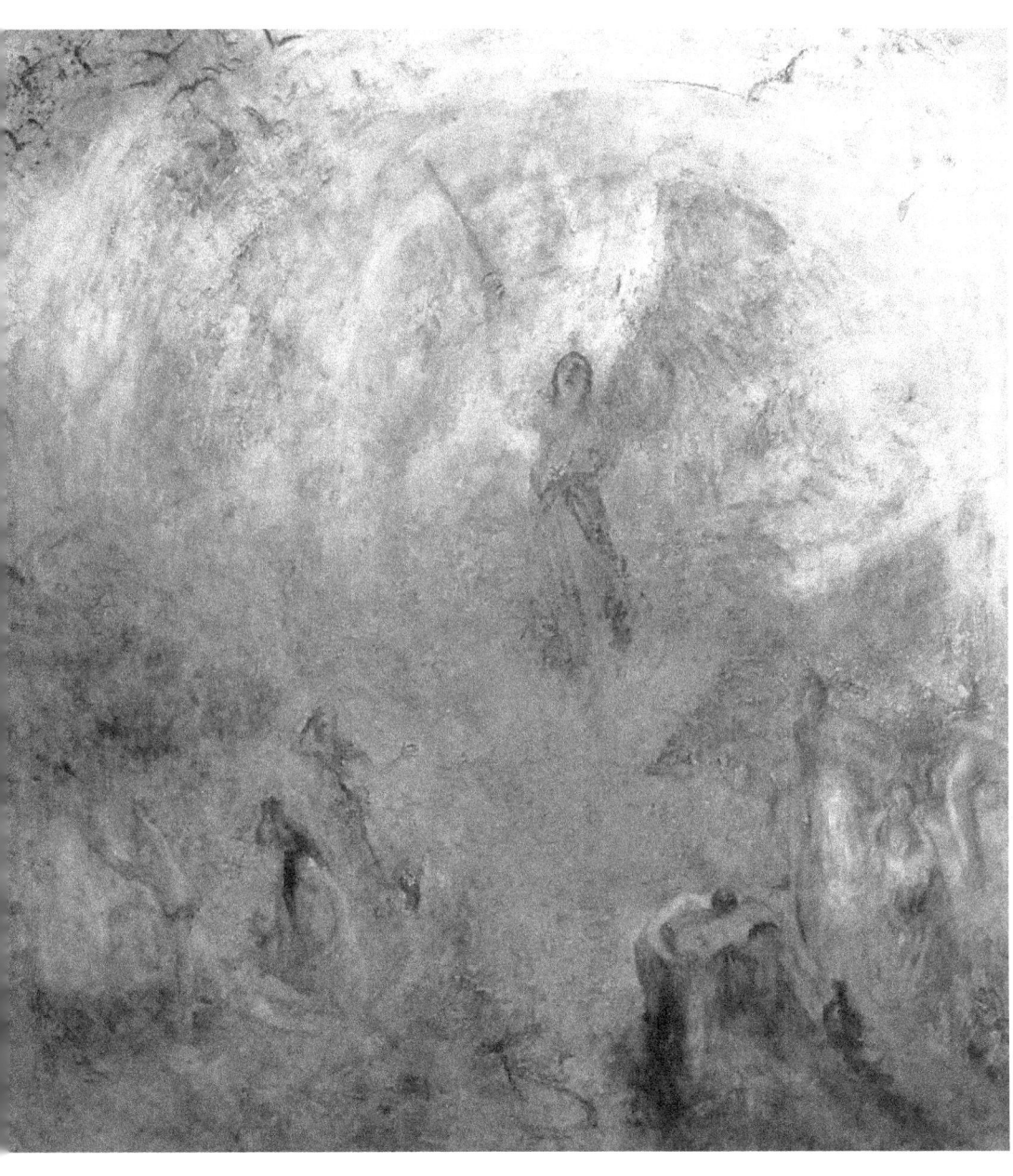

J.M.W. Turner, The Angel Standing In the Sun, 1846, Clore Gallery

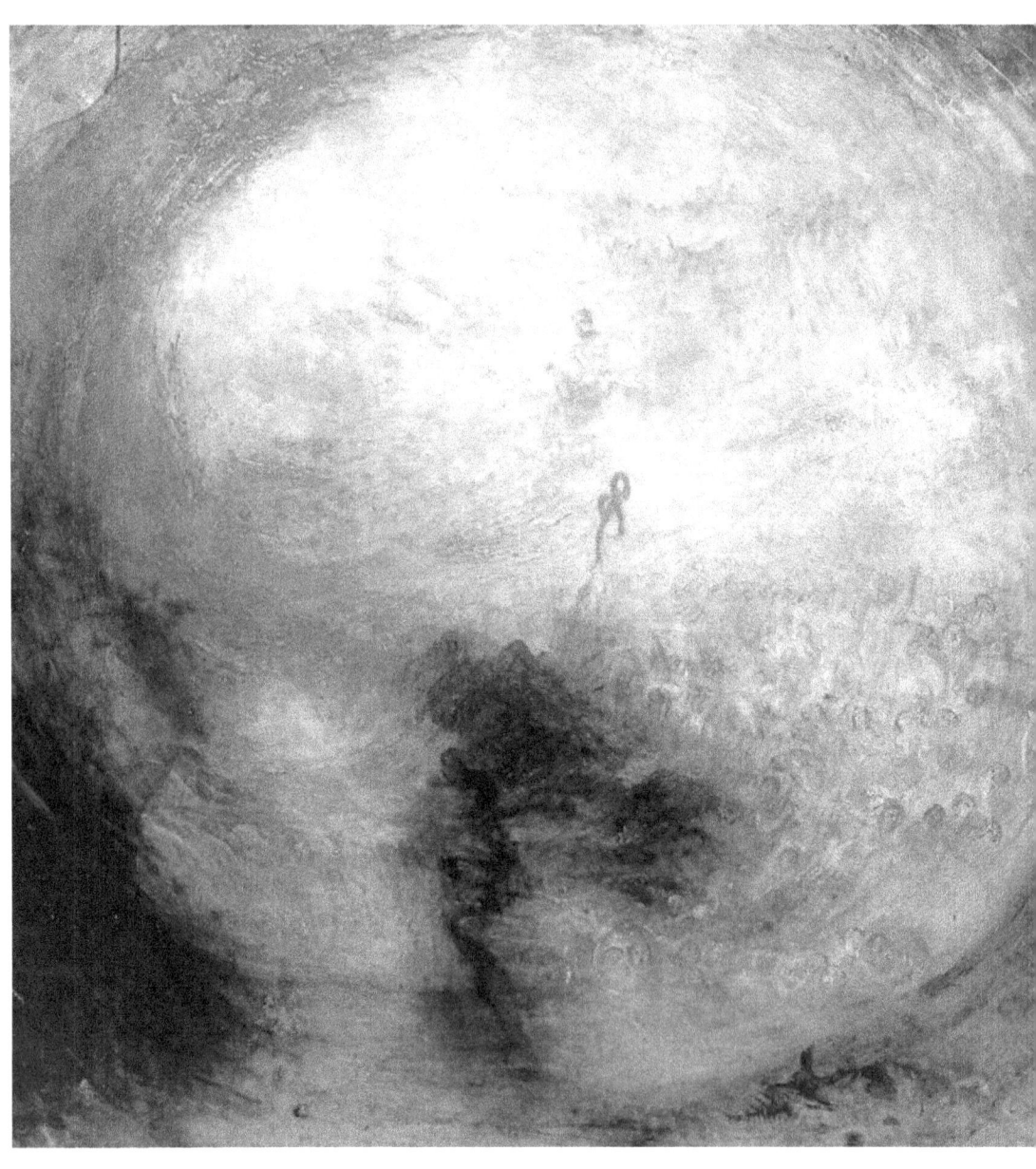

J.M.W. Turner, Light and Colour (Goethe's Theory),
The Morning After the Deluge, 1843, Clore Gallery

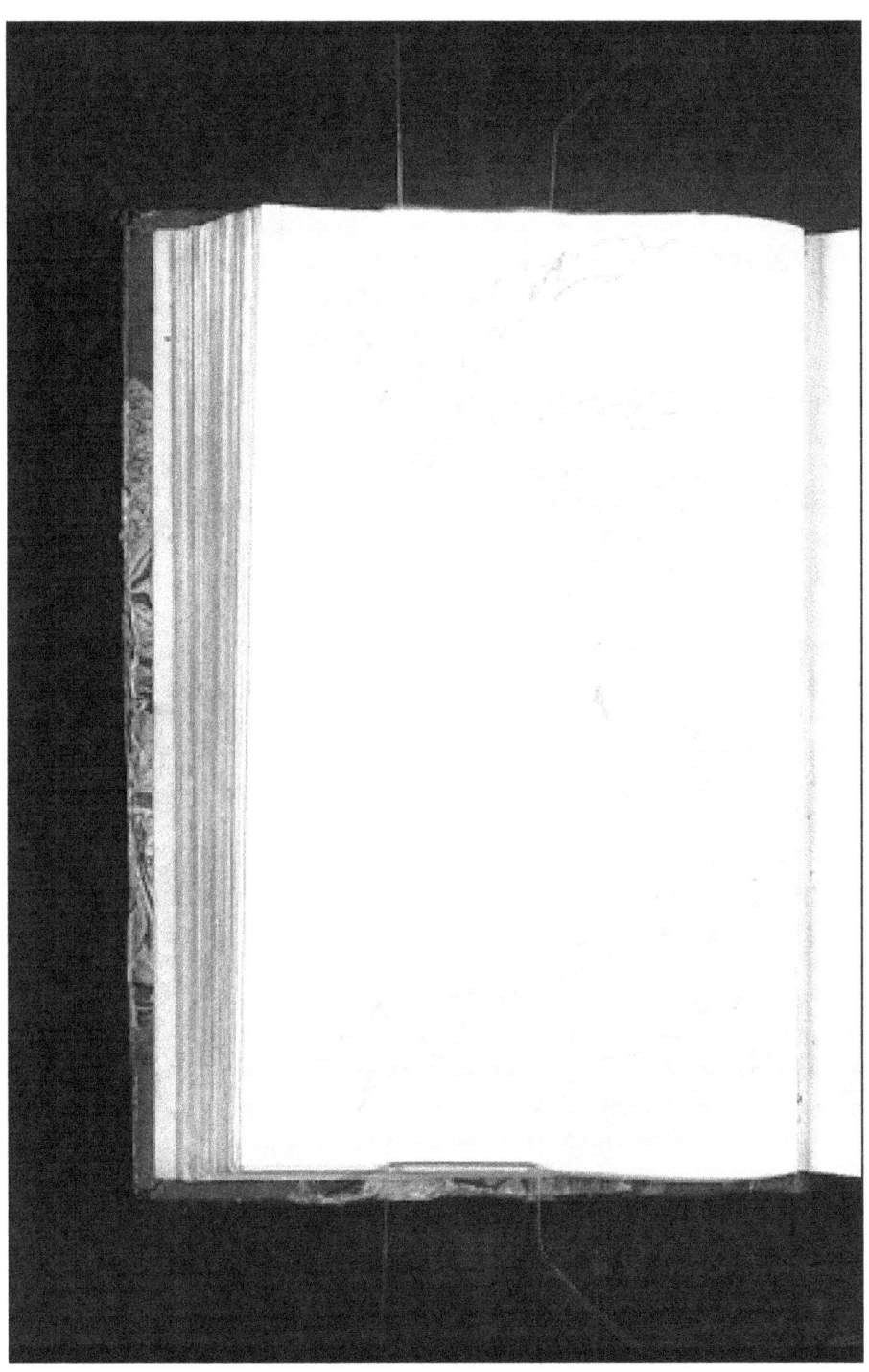

J.M.W. Turner, page from a sketchbook

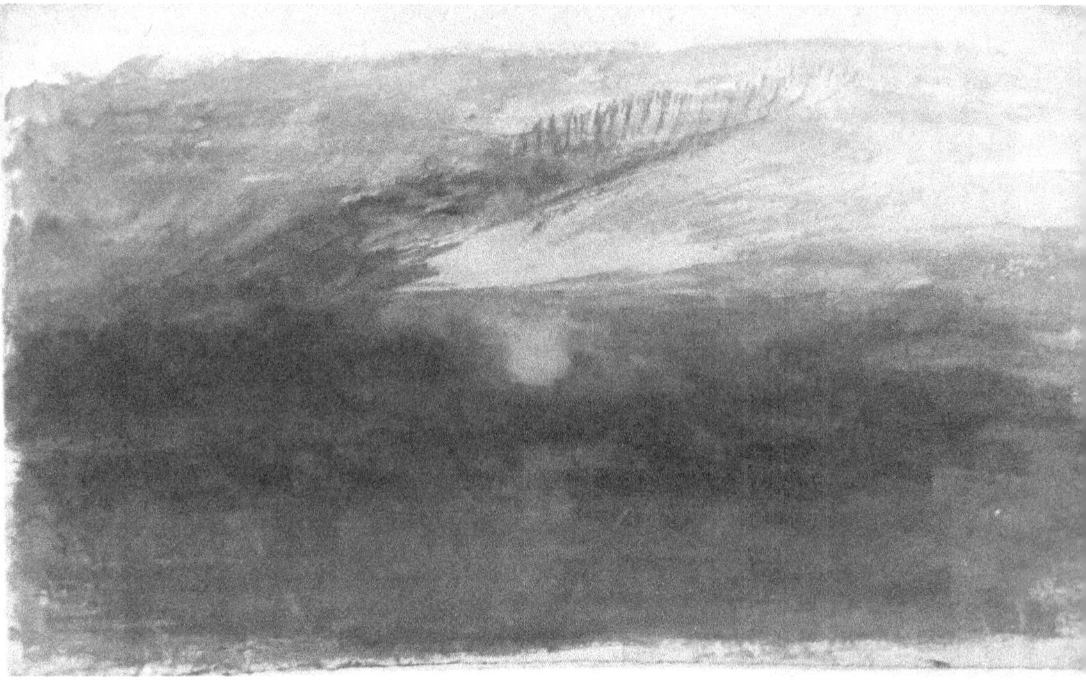

J.M.W. Turner, The Sun Setting, c. 1826 (top).
Crimson Sunset, 1823-30 (above). Both Clore Gallery.

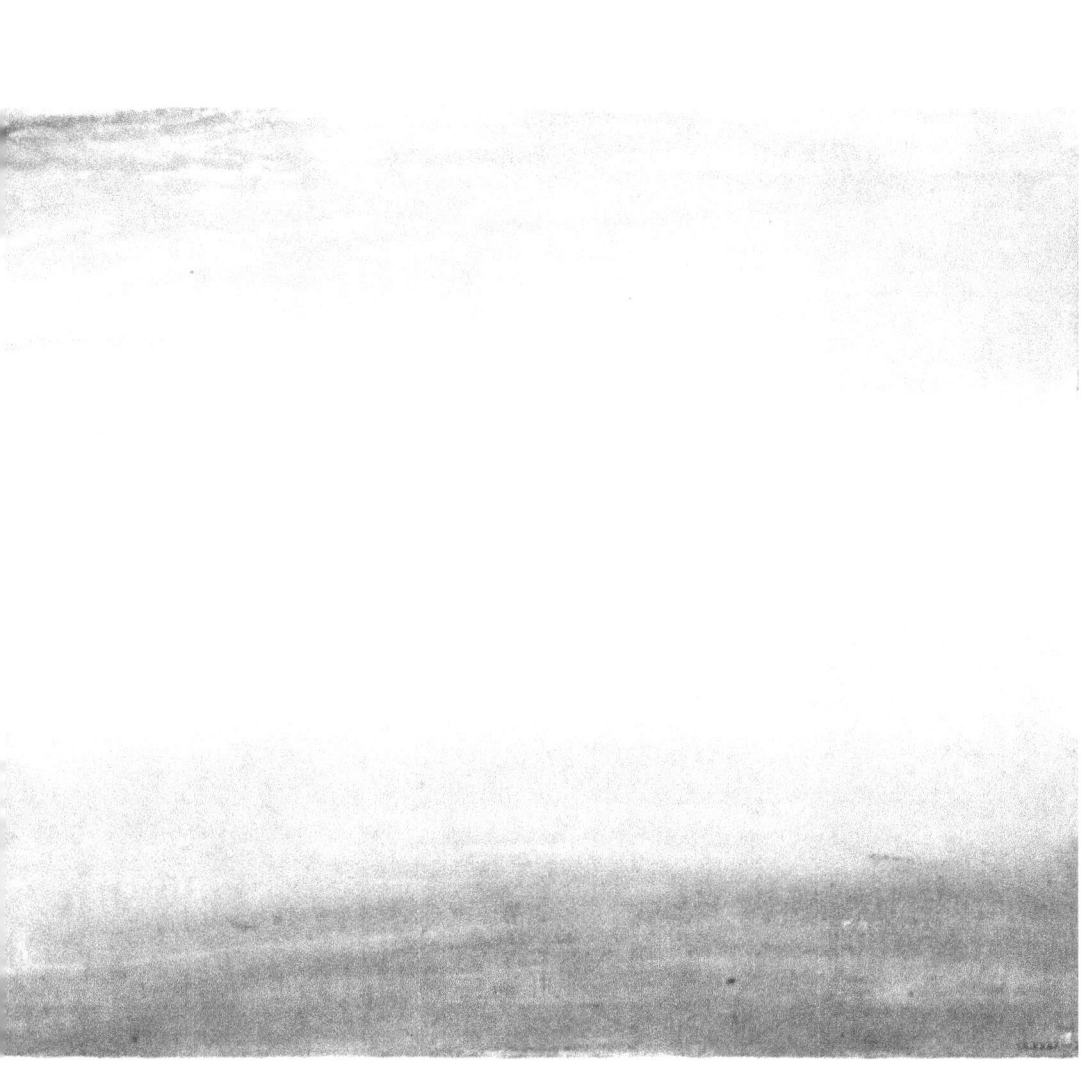

J.M.W. Turner, Colour Beginning, 1819

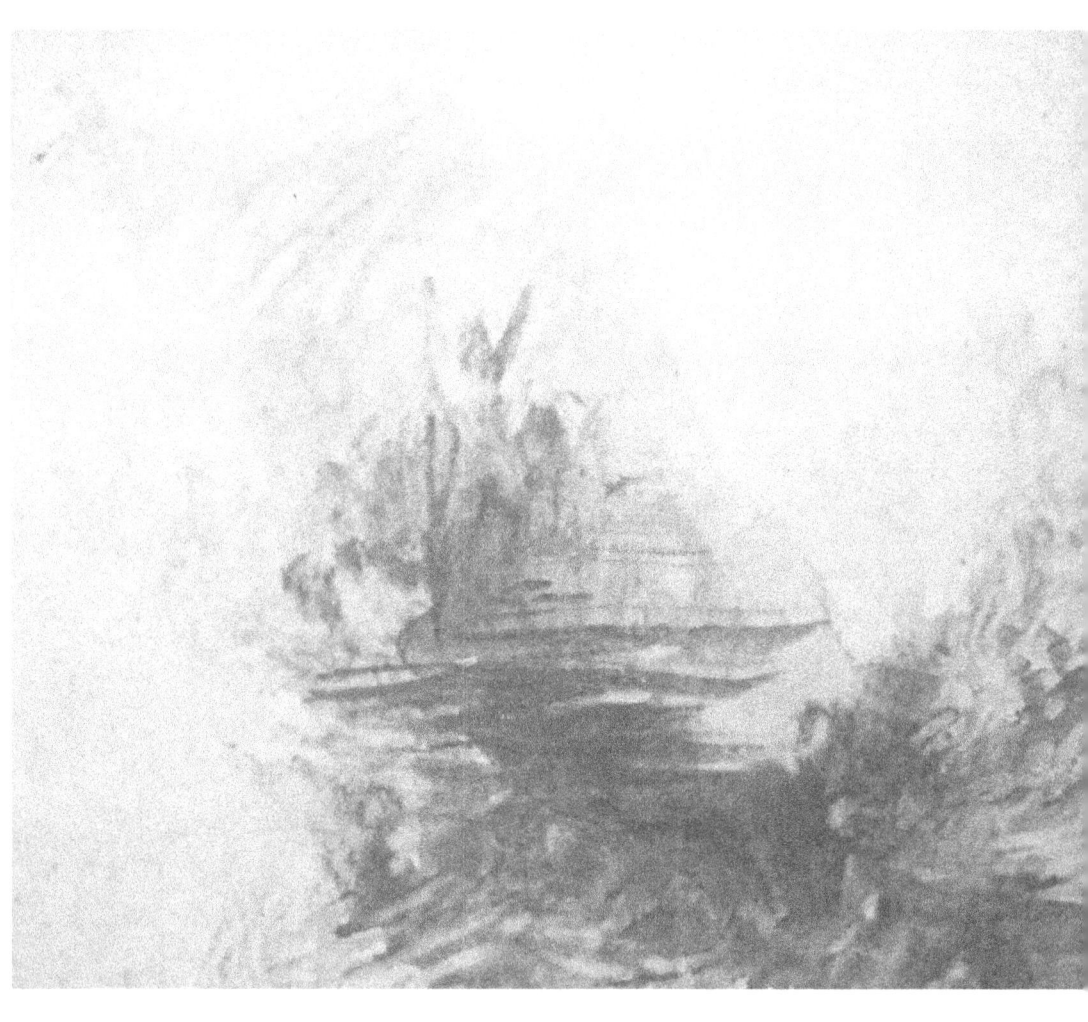

J.M.W. Turner, Satan Addressing His Angels, 1834, Clore Gallery

NOTES ON WORKS

A SHIP AGROUND.

From the oil painting by Turner in the Tate Gallery.

This beautiful sea piece is essentially Turner – the result of his personal observation. It was painted after he had freed himself from the desire to rival and outvie his predecessors, and before he became obsessed by the passion to paint pure sunlight. "A Ship Aground" is a pendant to "The Old Chain Pier, Brighton," which also hangs in the Tate Gallery.

HASTINGS.

(From the oil painting by Turner in the Tate Gallery)

One of the so-called "unfinished" pictures that, after half a century of seclusion in the cellars of the National Gallery, were removed to the Tate Gallery, and opened to public inspection early in February 1906. This great "find," as it was called, of twenty-one Turners was the sensation of the year in art circles. Hastings was a favourite subject with Turner.

NORHAM CASTLE.

(From the oil painting by Turner in the Tate Gallery)

One of the most beautiful of the impressionistic Turners that were removed from the cellars of the National Gallery early in 1906, cleaned, and hung in the Turner Room at Millbank. Once, when passing Norham Castle, Turner took off his hat to the ruins. His companion inquired the reason. "I made a drawing or painting of Norham Castle several years since," answered Turner. "It took; and from that day to this I have had as much to do as my hands could execute."

THE FIGHTING TÉMÉRAIRE.

(From the oil painting by Turner in the National Gallery)

Exhibited at the Royal Academy in 1839. In the previous year a party of friends, including Turner, were bound for Greenwich by water. They passed a steam-tug towing a superannuated battleship. "That's a fine subject for you, Turner." said Stanfield. The painter took the hint, and produced "The Fighting Téméraire tugged to her last Berth to be broken up."

VENICE: GRAND CANAL (SUNSET)

(From the water-colour by Turner in the National Gallery)

This twilight impression of the Grand Canal is one of the twenty Venice water-colours catalogued and described by Ruskin, and arranged by him for exhibition in the rooms on the ground floor of the National Gallery. "Turner's entirely final manner" he calls it "A noble sketch; injured by some change which has taken place in the coarse dark touches on the extreme left."

ARTH FROM THE LAKE OF ZUG.

(From the water-colour by Turner in the National Gallery)

"Elaborate and lovely," wrote Ruskin. "We sleep at Arth, and are up, and out on the lake, early in the morning; to good purpose. The sun rises behind the Mythens, and we see such an effect of lake and light, as we shall not forget soon."

LAUSANNE.

(From the water-colour by Turner in the National Gallery)

It may be Lausanne: it may be Berne, or merely a Turnerian Swiss dream of flushed spires, and a dim foreground where anything may be happening. This is one of the water-colours permanently on view at the National Gallery. The others are preserved in two large cabinets in an inner room, and shown in detachments at intervals of three months.

TIVOLI.

(From the oil painting by Turner in the Tate Gallery)

An imaginative classical landscape probably painted as a pendant to the "Arch of Constantine, Rome," which also hangs in the Tate Gallery. It has been suggested that the phantom figures are Tobit and the Angel. The setting suggests the scenery of Tivoli; but when Turner's imagination was fired, he cared little about topographical or historical accuracy.

MAURICE SENDAK

& the art of children's book illustration

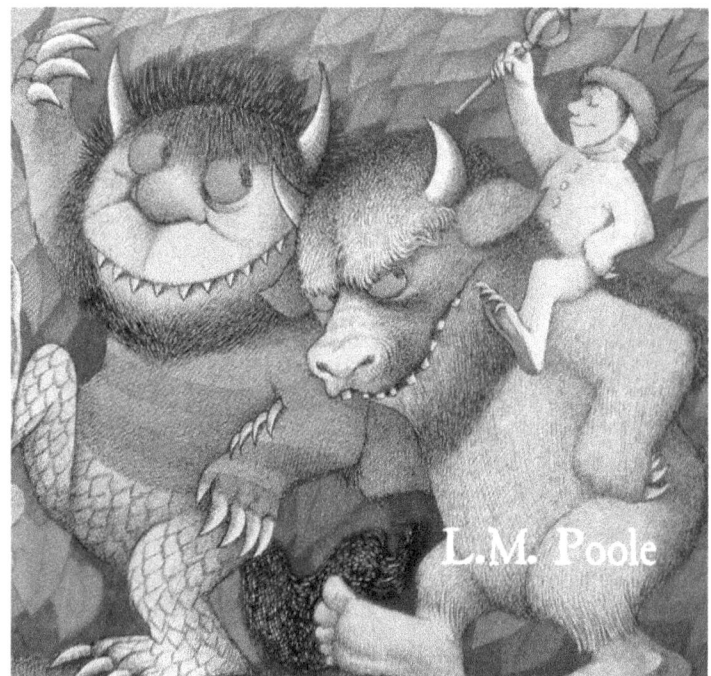

L.M. Poole

Maurice Sendak is the widely acclaimed American children's book author and
illustrator. This critical study focuses on his famous trilogy, *Where the Wild Things Are*,
In the Night Kitchen and *Outside Over There*, as well as the early works and Sendak's
superb depictions of the Grimm Brothers' fairy tales in *The Juniper Tree*. L.M. Poole
begins with a chapter on children's book illustration, in particular the treatment of
fairy tales. Sendak's work is situated within the history of children's book illustration,
and he is compared with many contemporary authors.

Fully illustrated. The book has been revised and updated for this edition.

ISBN 9781861714282 Pbk   ISBN 9781861713469 Hbk

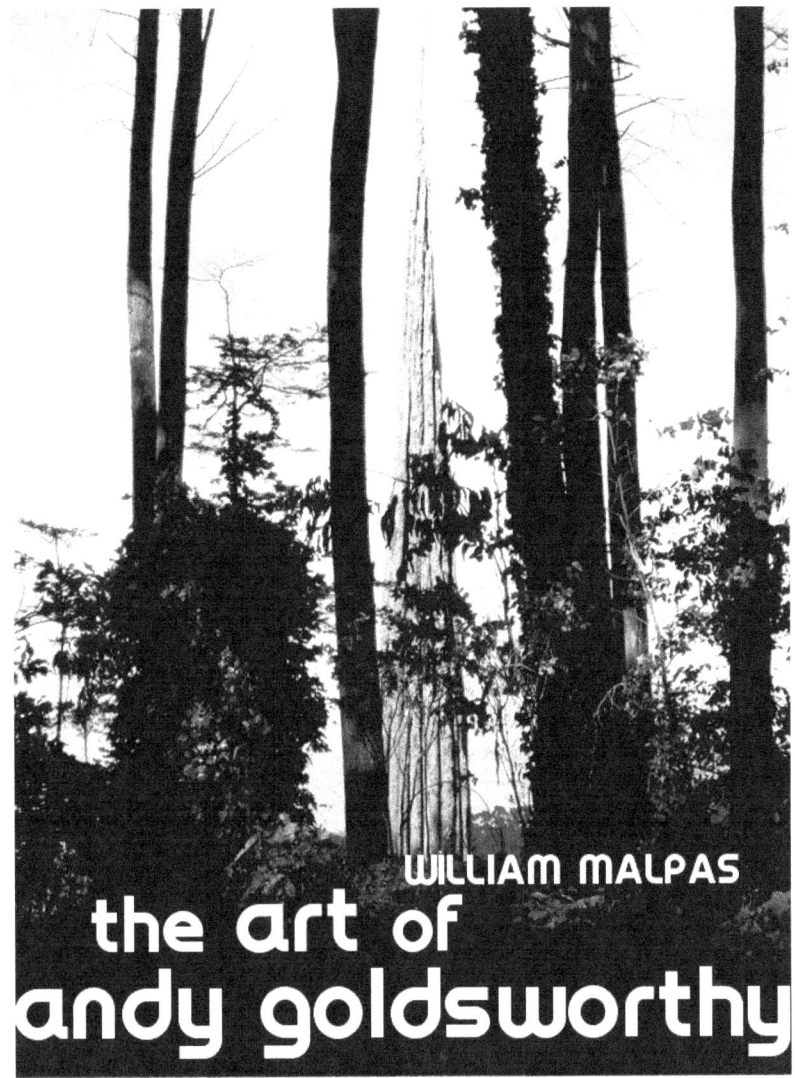

WILLIAM MALPAS
the art of
andy goldsworthy

This is the most comprehensive and detailed account of the art of Andy Goldsworthy available.

This study of Andy Goldsworthy discusses all of Goldsworthy's major exhibitions, books and projects, including the *Sheepfolds* project; *Garden of Stones* in New York; TV and dance collaborations; and the books *Wood, Stone, Time* and *Passage*. William Malpas surveys all of Goldsworthy's output, and analyzes his relation with other land artists such as Robert Smithson, the Christos, Walter de Maria, Chris Drury, Richard Long and David Nash; women sculptors; sculpture in the modern era; and Goldsworthy's place in the contemporary British art scene.

The book has been updated and revised for this new edition.

ISBN 9781861714107 Pbk   ISBN 9781861714114 Hbk
Fully illustrated   www.crmoon.com

CRESCENT MOON PUBLISHING

web: www.crmoon.com e-mail: cresmopub@yahoo.co.uk

ARTS, PAINTING, SCULPTURE

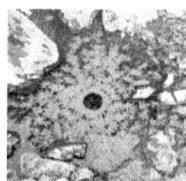

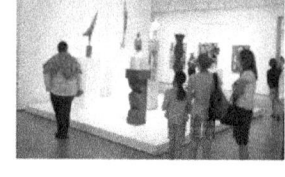

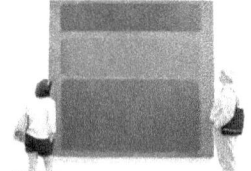

The Art of Andy Goldsworthy
Andy Goldsworthy: Touching Nature
Andy Goldsworthy in Close-Up
Andy Goldsworthy: Pocket Guide
Andy Goldsworthy In America
Land Art: A Complete Guide
The Art of Richard Long
Richard Long: Pocket Guide
Land Art In the UK
Land Art in Close-Up
Land Art In the U.S.A.
Land Art: Pocket Guide
Installation Art in Close-Up
Minimal Art and Artists In the 1960s and After
Colourfield Painting
Land Art DVD, TV documentary
Andy Goldsworthy DVD, TV documentary
The Erotic Object: Sexuality in Sculpture From Prehistory to the Present Day
Sex in Art: Pornography and Pleasure in Painting and Sculpture
Postwar Art
Sacred Gardens: The Garden in Myth, Religion and Art
Glorification: Religious Abstraction in Renaissance and 20th Century Art
Early Netherlandish Painting
Leonardo da Vinci
Piero della Francesca
Giovanni Bellini
Fra Angelico: Art and Religion in the Renaissance
Mark Rothko: The Art of Transcendence
Frank Stella: American Abstract Artist
Jasper Johns
Brice Marden
Alison Wilding: The Embrace of Sculpture
Vincent van Gogh: Visionary Landscapes
Eric Gill: Nuptials of God
Constantin Brancusi: Sculpting the Essence of Things
Max Beckmann
Caravaggio
Gustave Moreau
Egon Schiele: Sex and Death In Purple Stockings
Delizioso Fotografico Fervore: Works In Process 1
Sacro Cuore: Works In Process 2
The Light Eternal: J.M.W. Turner
The Madonna Glorified: Karen Arthurs

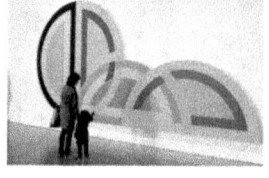

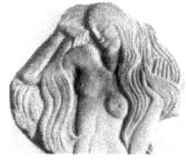

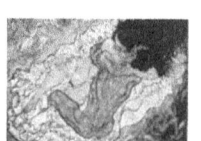

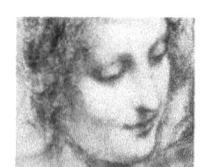

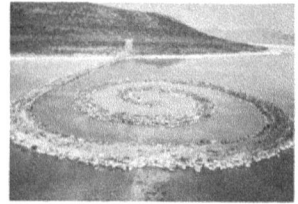

LITERATURE

J.R.R. Tolkien: The Books, The Films, The Whole Cultural Phenomenon
J.R.R. Tolkien: Pocket Guide
Tolkien's Heroic Quest
The *Earthsea* Books of Ursula Le Guin
Beauties, Beasts and Enchantment: Classic French Fairy Tales
German Popular Stories by the Brothers Grimm
Philip Pullman and *His Dark Materials*
Sexing Hardy: Thomas Hardy and Feminism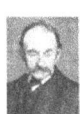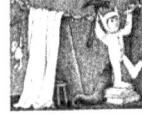
Thomas Hardy's *Tess of the d'Urbervilles*
Thomas Hardy's *Jude the Obscure*
Thomas Hardy: The Tragic Novels
Love and Tragedy: Thomas Hardy
The Poetry of Landscape in Hardy
Wessex Revisited: Thomas Hardy and John Cowper Powys
Wolfgang Iser: Essays and Interviews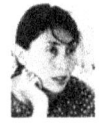
Petrarch, Dante and the Troubadours
Maurice Sendak and the Art of Children's Book Illustration
Andrea Dworkin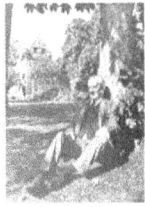
Cixous, Irigaray, Kristeva: The *Jouissance* of French Feminism
Julia Kristeva: Art, Love, Melancholy, Philosophy, Semiotics and Psychoanalysis
Hélène Cixous I Love You: The *Jouissance* of Writing
Luce Irigaray: Lips, Kissing, and the Politics of Sexual Difference
Peter Redgrove: Here Comes the Flood
Peter Redgrove: Sex-Magic-Poetry-Cornwall
Lawrence Durrell: Between Love and Death, East and West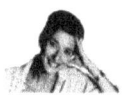
Love, Culture & Poetry: Lawrence Durrell
Cavafy: Anatomy of a Soul
German Romantic Poetry: Goethe, Novalis, Heine, Hölderlin
Feminism and Shakespeare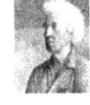
Shakespeare: Love, Poetry & Magic
The Passion of D.H. Lawrence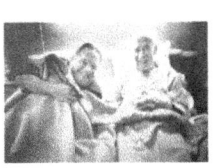
D.H. Lawrence: Symbolic Landscapes
D.H. Lawrence: Infinite Sensual Violence
Rimbaud: Arthur Rimbaud and the Magic of Poetry
The Ecstasies of John Cowper Powys
Sensualism and Mythology: The Wessex Novels of John Cowper Powys
Amorous Life: John Cowper Powys and the Manifestation of Affectivity (H.W. Fawkner)
Postmodern Powys: New Essays on John Cowper Powys (Joe Boulter)
Rethinking Powys: Critical Essays on John Cowper Powys
Paul Bowles & Bernardo Bertolucci
Rainer Maria Rilke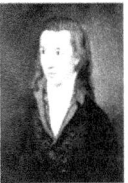
Joseph Conrad: *Heart of Darkness*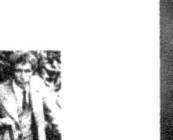
In the Dim Void: Samuel Beckett
Samuel Beckett Goes into the Silence
André Gide: Fiction and Fervour
Jackie Collins and the Blockbuster Novel
Blinded By Her Light: The Love-Poetry of Robert Graves
The Passion of Colours: Travels In Mediterranean Lands
Poetic Forms

POETRY

Ursula Le Guin: Walking In Cornwall
Peter Redgrove: Here Comes The Flood
Peter Redgrove: Sex-Magic-Poetry-Cornwall
Dante: Selections From the Vita Nuova
Petrarch, Dante and the Troubadours
William Shakespeare: Sonnets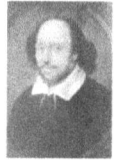
William Shakespeare: Complete Poems
Blinded By Her Light: The Love-Poetry of Robert Graves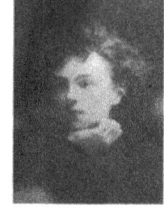
Emily Dickinson: Selected Poems
Emily Brontë: Poems
Thomas Hardy: Selected Poems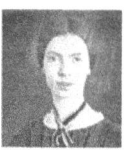
Percy Bysshe Shelley: Poems
John Keats: Selected Poems
John Keats: Poems of 1820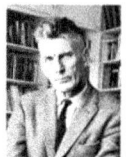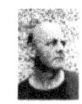
D.H. Lawrence: Selected Poems
Edmund Spenser: Poems
Edmund Spenser: Amoretti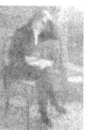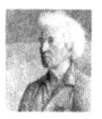
John Donne: Poems
Henry Vaughan: Poems
Sir Thomas Wyatt: Poems
Robert Herrick: Selected Poems
Rilke: Space, Essence and Angels in the Poetry of Rainer Maria Rilke
Rainer Maria Rilke: Selected Poems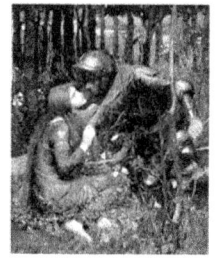
Friedrich Hölderlin: Selected Poems
Arseny Tarkovsky: Selected Poems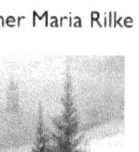
Arthur Rimbaud: Selected Poems
Arthur Rimbaud: A Season in Hell
Arthur Rimbaud and the Magic of Poetry
Novalis: Hymns To the Night
German Romantic Poetry
Paul Verlaine: Selected Poems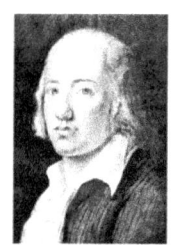
Elizaethan Sonnet Cycles
D.J. Enright: By-Blows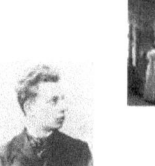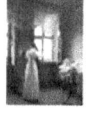
Jeremy Reed: Brigitte's Blue Heart
Jeremy Reed: Claudia Schiffer's Red Shoes
Gorgeous Little Orpheus
Radiance: New Poems
Crescent Moon Book of Nature Poetry
Crescent Moon Book of Love Poetry
Crescent Moon Book of Mystical Poetry
Crescent Moon Book of Elizabethan Love Poetry
Crescent Moon Book of Metaphysical Poetry
Crescent Moon Book of Romantic Poetry
Pagan America: New American Poetry

MEDIA, CINEMA, FEMINISM and CULTURAL STUDIES

J.R.R. Tolkien: The Books, The Films, The Whole Cultural Phenomenon
J.R.R. Tolkien: Pocket Guide
The *Lord of the Rings* Movies: Pocket Guide
The Cinema of Hayao Miyazaki
Hayao Miyazaki: *Princess Mononoke*: Pocket Movie Guide
Hayao Miyazaki: *Spirited Away*: Pocket Movie Guide
Tim Burton : Hallowe'en For Hollywood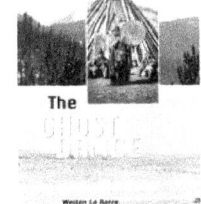
Ken Russell
Ken Russell: *Tommy*: Pocket Movie Guide
The Ghost Dance: The Origins of Religion
The Peyote Cult
Cixous, Irigaray, Kristeva: The *Jouissance* of French Feminism
Julia Kristeva: Art, Love, Melancholy, Philosophy, Semiotics and Psychoanalysis
Luce Irigaray: Lips, Kissing, and the Politics of Sexual Difference
Hélène Cixous I Love You: The *Jouissance* of Writing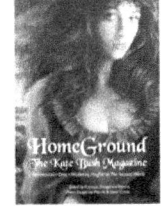
Andrea Dworkin
'Cosmo Woman': The World of Women's Magazines
Women in Pop Music
HomeGround: The Kate Bush Anthology
Discovering the Goddess (Geoffrey Ashe)
The Poetry of Cinema
The Sacred Cinema of Andrei Tarkovsky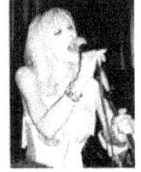
Andrei Tarkovsky: Pocket Guide
Andrei Tarkovsky: *Mirror*: Pocket Movie Guide
Andrei Tarkovsky: *The Sacrifice*: Pocket Movie Guide
Walerian Borowczyk: Cinema of Erotic Dreams
Jean-Luc Godard: The Passion of Cinema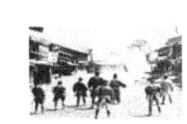
Jean-Luc Godard: *Hail Mary*: Pocket Movie Guide
Jean-Luc Godard: *Contempt*: Pocket Movie Guide
Jean-Luc Godard: *Pierrot le Fou*: Pocket Movie Guide
John Hughes and Eighties Cinema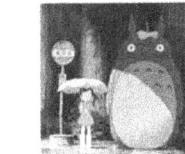
Ferris Bueller's Day Off: Pocket Movie Guide
Jean-Luc Godard: Pocket Guide
The Cinema of Richard Linklater
Liv Tyler: Star In Ascendance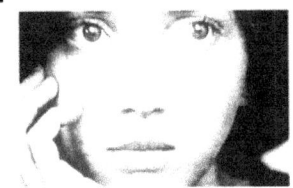
Blade Runner and the Films of Philip K. Dick
Paul Bowles and Bernardo Bertolucci
Media Hell: Radio, TV and the Press
An Open Letter to the BBC
Detonation Britain: Nuclear War in the UK
Feminism and Shakespeare
Wild Zones: Pornography, Art and Feminism
Sex in Art: Pornography and Pleasure in Painting and Sculpture
Sexing Hardy: Thomas Hardy and Feminism

The Light Eternal is a model monograph, an exemplary job. The subject matter of the book is beautifully
organised and dead on beam. (Lawrence Durrell)
It is amazing for me to see my work treated with such passion and respect. (Andrea Dworkin)

CRESCENT MOON PUBLISHING
P.O. Box 1312, Maidstone, Kent, ME14 5XU, Great Britain. www.crmoon.com

cresmopub@yahoo.co.uk   www.crescentmoon.org.uk